I0797731

WHAT DOESN'T KILL ME MAKES ME WEIRDER AND HARDER TO RELATE TO

WHAT DOESN'T KILL ME MAKES ME WEIRDER AND HARDER TO RELATE TO

A MEMOIR

MARY LUCIA

UNIVERSITY OF MINNESOTA PRESS
Minneapolis
London

Published by the University of Minnesota Press
111 Third Avenue South, Suite 290
Minneapolis, MN 55401-2520
http://www.upress.umn.edu

ISBN 978-1-5179-1886-6

A Cataloging-in-Publication record for this book is available from the Library of Congress.

Book design by Endpaper Studio
Typeset in Amira 2 and Dante MT

Printed in Canada on acid-free paper

34 33 32 31 30 29 28 27 26 25 10 9 8 7 6 5 4 3 2 1

The holy trinity.

Smudge, Crash, and Lefty.

CONTENTS

As someone who has been on the other side of Mary Lucia's microphone, I can say that her intimate candor, wit, and encyclopedic rock and roll knowledge made me feel completely at ease and as if I were with an old friend, even though we had just met. These qualities of hers didn't extend only to those seated at her in-studio microphone—the same thing I felt was felt by her vast radio audience. That's why she was such a beloved radio personality for so many years. They were listening to a trusted friend.

As she notes in these pages, it's often pointed out that certain dangers can come with being in the public eye. But is it the responsibility of said public personality to accept a life of terror? Is that an acceptable price for displaying such an honest, vulnerable, human voice? A simple "thank you" would suffice!

Given that I too grew up in an eccentric family, I get great comfort hearing the often hilarious but sad tales of familial dysfunction Mary unwittingly was brought into. I mean, what family isn't dysfunctional? But we're talking about a notable case here, I'd say.

That Mary manages to tell her harrowing tale with such humor and make such an entertaining book out of it is a testament to the personality I have spoken of. Read it and weep. And laugh. And weep a couple more times. And laugh even a few times more.

Mark Oliver Everett, author of
Things the Grandchildren Should Know

PROLOGUE
Smudge

I LIKE ANIMALS MORE THAN PEOPLE.

As long as I can remember I've wanted a Pug. Having been bred primarily for companionship to Chinese royalty and not equipped with traditional mad skills, they're ridiculous and unique. Hard to train, hilarious, and with personality to spare. Sounded like a perfect match for me.

The relationship I was in for most of my late twenties to late thirties was with a man who had great hair and was a talented songwriter who loved cats as much as I did. Score. However, the mere mention of my longing for a squishy-faced canine was met with a disapproving look and sigh. Since when did he become my father? I held out hope that if he loved me enough, surely, he would cave to my desire.

One year my birthday card included a handwritten note from him that was "Good for one Pug." My heart strings were shredded. He did love and understand me as much as I thought. Immediately I began the search for adoption.

Mind you, these beautiful specimens don't grow on trees, but wouldn't that be dope if they did? Many flaming hoops of metaphorical dog shit needed jumping through, lots of vetting and applications. I think it was easier being accepted to NYU than it was to locate and be approved for a Pug.

I found one in Minnesota and made the proper inquiries; things were starting to roll. When I shared the news with the beau, he curtly told me, "I've changed my mind." What was I, eight years old? Being a giver by nature it hit me like a sucker punch. The result of that warped way of minimizing your own needs translates quite simply: Ask For Nothing. Get Nothing. I'd never expect unconditional love from another person.

In hindsight that relationship worked until it didn't.

LIVING ON MY OWN for the first time in a decade, I naturally resumed the search for my heart's desire: a man that was giving and supportive. Fook no. A Pug.

I found a woman in Hick Stick, Minnesota, who had a pregnant Fawn Pug. I immediately put that unseen fetus on layaway. I also went out to meet the breeder and fell in love with the expectant Mama. She was still a few weeks away from giving birth, and not unlike any pregnant woman she was dragging her tits looking for a spot of shade and dreaming of her next cocktail.

I was at work when I got the call that she had her litter. But I could tell from the tone in her voice somehow I was going to be disappointed once again. She explained that she had one less pup than expected and the rest were all spoken for. Impossible to make pleasantries, I congratulated her and expressed my chagrin when unexpectedly my voice cracked. Then tears. She asked if she could phone me back, and again my heart jumped thinking that maybe one of the spoken-for puppies was being held for an adopter that might not go through. Ten minutes later she called and said, "I saw how well you bonded with the mother. I'd be willing to let you adopt her." Without hesitation I said I would love nothing more.

Breeders usually get lazy when naming dogs, and truthfully, I knew I'd be changing her name from whatever the hell it was originally. Heidi? Princess? Smudge was mine. She'd have to finish weaning the pups before I could bring her home.

The day I rescued her, and I do say *rescue,* she was sitting in a pen on the classified section of the *Star Tribune,* three puppies climbing on her when we exchanged a look. Hers was, Get me out of this fucking brothel. Mine was complete empathy.

So began our beautiful life together. The real estate of my heart had expanded acres. She went everywhere with me. Anyone I loved she loved. My best friend, Jess, and I would drink wine and have dress-up parties in which Smudge modeled an array of fetching frocks and Halloween costumes simply for our enjoyment. Nobody could rock a French maid outfit with a giant gut like my girl.

In my job as a radio host, I play music, but talking about my love for my fur family is as much a part of who I am as the obsessive nature for my love of rock and roll. I shared the whole story of Smudge with listeners. How is it possible to get exactly what you want? And ultimately, who rescued whom?

Smudge had her own social media page; I would have her pose ridiculous questions online. I believed her to be a deep thinker and social anthropologist. People responded. She became The People's Pug. I realized I was sharing more of my personal life than I had previously in all my years on radio. There was a new sense of connection I had to strangers. People shared their own stories of dog life with me. The funny, inquisitive—and naturally—the gut-ripping pain of loss.

I had quite an arsenal of songs at the ready for a heartbroken listener who had to put their fur child to sleep. By far the hardest part as pet parents is that we choose to unconditionally love an animal whose life is knowingly far more temporary than ours, and this comes with the impossible decision to make end-of-life plans. I was painfully experienced here, having done this my entire life with my beloved cats. I tried to offer comfort by validating a listener's grief, having questionable Mobbed-up relatives even offering a mercy whack.

When I first noticed Smudge having difficulty with her back legs, I felt as though I had swallowed a shot glass. Something was not right. We both knew it. Smudge, being a willing participant in all ways that extended joy to myself and others, seemed almost a little embarrassed. Not unlike me: not wanting to draw concern or attention to something painful. Might be easier to incorporate this atrophy into a jaunty new swagger.

X-rays showed an arachnoid tumor on her precious little spine. Which meant it was spread out like a spider. Surgery was the next step. I was willing to do anything for her as she had been so selfless toward me and my unconventional proclivities. Surgery was scheduled for my birthday, August 6. I took the week off from work to be at home for her recovery. The veterinary surgeon left a message after the procedure saying the words no one wants to hear: "We got as much of the tumor as we could."

I was so consumed with doing whatever needed to be done that I had failed to examine what recovery for an older dog would look like. If there was any question of how tough the road would be, it was answered when the vet tech led my beautiful Smudge out to the front waiting area diapered with a sling under her tummy, her back legs dragging lifelessly behind her. Holy Christ, she can't walk on her own. This was ten thousand times worse than before her surgery. What had I done? I paid the exorbitant bill with money I didn't have and carried her to my VW Bug. Pug in a Bug.

A crash course in mastering diapering and sling-walking commenced as soon as we got home. I also bought a lime green stroller for her. Nothing was going to keep us from our twice-daily walks. Just like her easygoing self she seemed thoroughly happy to be a passenger; beaming from her new whip, we greeted neighbors all expecting to see my "baby" met with a look of confusion at her shaved back bearing a huge Frankenstein set of stitches.

Weekly aqua therapy began immediately. Every Tuesday after I got off air at 6 p.m., I had to hightail her to the rehab clinic. She walked on a water treadmill for ten minutes while I stood in wading boots in front of her, encouraging her like a loaf of bread slowly moving down the conveyer belt at Cub Foods. We did this for eleven months and there was some improvement, and the sling was no longer needed. She now ate lying on the floor in front of her dish. Stairs were a thing of the past, but carrying her up and down was a small price to pay. All of this I shared with my listeners. The setbacks, the milestones, and the absurdity. People of The Current were Team Smudge all the way.

One morning the following July she couldn't get up from a sleeping position. No vet had to tell me what was happening. That lethal tumor had grown back, which I knew was always a possibility. I lay on the floor nose to snout with Smudge and we had a long conversation. I thanked her profusely for all the effort put forth in rehab. I begged for forgiveness if this last year had been selfish on my part. I told her she changed my life. I explained she never had to do anything uncomfortable just to please me; I gave her a thousand baby kisses and whispered that, most important, she showed me what unconditional love felt like for the first time. She let rip a noxious fart, which I took to be her final absolution of my deeds.

The day before she went to heaven I worked and thought about nothing but the next day's life-changing appointment. I knew I would tell our story and reveal its final chapter on air. People had been with us throughout our ride-or-die friendship. I ugly-cried on air and gasped a few words about the following day's duties, how devastated I was. I played Debussy's *Clair de Lune,* the most beautiful and saddest song I know. I've never heard anyone cry live on air other than myself, and I can't imagine what that sounds like to a listener of a rock station.

The outpouring of understanding humbled me to my core. People seemed to genuinely appreciate the vulnerability of my leaving a few vital organs on the soundboard that afternoon. People I'd never met offered a personal strength that I had never received from family. Smudge's last day in her broken body was lying on the floor at the vet eating a chocolate ice cream sundae. Yes, I said *chocolate.* Fade to everlasting snoring and freedom.

The following week I tried to keep up with the condolences that poured in via email at work. A man messaged me saying that he too had lost his dog recently and that he was having a tough time. I'm sure my response was genuine and empathetic. Doing what comes naturally to me, responding to a stranger's pain was not unusual. But I could never have predicted that this small gesture, a simple response to a stranger that I had done thousands of times over my career, would unfold into the most terrifying three years of my life. I would never feel safe again.

INTRODUCTION
Please Allow Me to Introduce Myself

I WANT YOU TO KNOW WHAT YOU'RE GETTING INTO. THIS IS MY STORY, and so to preserve my sanity and yours, I've decided to include other chapters about my life to break up the shit show of being stalked. Yes, for three years I was paralyzed with fear, but life goes on around you, you do your job, pick up Q-tips at Target, worry about aging parents, pry half-dead mice from your cats' mouths, and that is what makes the juxtaposition of living with ongoing trauma unreal.

You don't know me. You might be thinking this book is filled with nothing but PTSD nightmares. Good lord, I promise you I wouldn't do that. Who would want to read that? Besides refusing to be defined by this maddening time in my life, I'd like to believe my imagination is stronger than the fear inflicted on me by a stranger.

It's not even a choice. It has to be.

Throughout those three years my life felt as if it weren't my own. I was more an observer than a willing participant, and the changes that were happening to the way I behaved were dictated by a complete stranger. At so many points I couldn't recognize myself. It's important to tell you that I have had a good sense of who I am since I was a kid. That certainly doesn't mean I haven't tripped and fallen, making reckless choices as I've gotten older.

But at my core some things remained unwavering. I was a creative kid and could entertain myself, no problem. I had a formidable awareness of how I wanted to dress. I seemed to possess a confidence that I hadn't yet earned. Innately, I valued things that were used and older to be more precious than something new.

I am always looking for my next great laugh. In times of serious unpleasant reality, I reach into a dark bag of tricks for levity.

Also, I have always written. Not in diary form. Short stories, letters, mini plays, and later, record reviews about my favorite music in my imaginary zine.

Whether I consciously knew I was writing a book during the three wretched years between 2013 and 2016 I can't say for certain. Something frantic was compelling me to document this, in the form of scribbled feelings and accounts in various notebooks. Like a trembling hand on a Ouija Board, the cursor moves almost separate from my own will.

It felt weighty and necessary, though I never thought of it as worthy until much later.

I'VE BEEN A ROCK RADIO DJ my entire adult life. You could say it's in my blood or at the very least in my stool.

Every day I wake up and think of the Rolling Stones and I don't think there's anything odd about that.

I can pick out the perfect Christmas tree in under ten seconds.

I dread everything. I regret nothing.

I'm certain I was born neck first.

The first time I did blow it was off a copy of *Thriller.*

I learned to drive in a cemetery.

I'll try anything twice.

When I was seven, I had to get rid of a single goldfish kept in a bowl in my bedroom because it was keeping me awake at night.

I court failure because the risk feels good.

Whenever someone I know moves, I ask how many bathrooms there are in the new house. Imagining two or more household members simultaneously having food poisoning is a big thing with me.

People attending NFL football games appear to be the most carefree human beings on Earth. Joyous and unrelatable, as if they have never had to pay a hospital bill or tell a family member to eff off at a holiday dinner.

No matter how great a movie plot, I completely tap out when there is a simulated protest scene. The overacting shouting sign-wielders categorically are the worst display of acting. I don't blame the extras because I know, off-camera, someone is yelling, "Angrier!"

While walking my dogs, I force myself to imagine the scenario of getting jumped and wonder if pent-up rage and lifelong anxiety will be enough to thwart and fight off attackers.

I am fascinated by stories of conjoined twins in which one twin is in a romantic relationship.

When meeting someone new, I'm immediately drawn closer if they swear randomly.

I once lived in a Victorian round room apartment. It didn't take long to acclimate to its uniqueness. I just needed to accept that no furniture was flush against any wall. Everything was jutting out awkwardly, ready for the perfect midnight toe stub. I thought and behaved in a less linear way during this time in my life, and I attribute it all to living in a spherical fun house.

I can understand the difference between someone who says, "I don't dance" and the person who says, "I don't know how to dance." I want to hug the latter.

Recognizing that a person who is reserved and economical with their words is not an a-hole has helped immensely in my career.

I once had a great shrink who taught me never to start a sentence with "If I'm being honest with you." It implies you're normally an insincere, big honkin' liar.

I've been playing lots of Insomnia Jeopardy at night. "I'll take people who've wronged me for $500, Alex." I know the best revenge is living well, but in the real world, healthy doses of spite never killed anyone.

I've used the expression "Touch 'em all, Kirby Puckett" in a sexual manner.

I compulsively cut every tag out of my clothing.

Only once in my life did I get a spray tan, which is maybe the most compromising physical position to be in in front of a stranger. When she began to make chitchat—which I'm certain they're advised to do when you're dropping it like it's hot—she asked if I had plans for the Fourth of July, which I found irrelevant and funny. I started in on a story about how a group of friends and I do historical reenactments at Fort Snelling. Powdered wigs, homemade musket rifles, etc. All this frivolity in a paper thong!

I never memorized any license plate number of any car I drove. But I can remember my childhood landline phone number: my mom was creative enough to set it to music on the piano and I sang it.

I would rather spend money on the highest-quality bedding than see a dentist about the raw nerve ending that's throbbing in my molar. My dental plan is I've been chewing on the right side exclusively going on four years.

I'm proud that I've maintained a sense of being game. By that I mean I am still up for trying something ridiculous. I grew up in a household where someone was frequently daring you to throw your wallet in the fireplace or eat dog food for twenty dollars. It all seemed pretty reasonable.

I once auditioned for a voice-over job where the written direction from the producer was "Think Mary Lucia-ish." I didn't get booked. I think I nailed the Mary Lucia. It was the "ish" where I stumbled.

I love the unnatural voice people adopt when talking on the phone to an automated system asking for their spoken preferences. The same strained voice is used when speaking into the TV remote. "In a few words, tell me what you need from Apple Support." There are never a few words that come coherently to mind—other than "Kill me now."

When asked, as a child, what my plans were for a Saturday afternoon, my usual response was "I'm going to pretend." Nothing's changed.

1
SPREADSHEETS AND SADNESS

COMING INTO THE WORLD OF GROUNDBREAKING COMMERCIAL alternative radio in Minneapolis in 1994, my career had started and peaked almost simultaneously.

Revolution Radio—REV105—was the first independently owned music station that played Soul Coughing, Revolting Cocks, Edith Piaf, and Elliott Smith. We were all music freaks in our early twenties and down for the cause. The station was presented with humor and a nod to our audiences' intelligence. The die-hard listeners who loved this radio programming were no joke and would have taken a bullet for this station to stay on-air. Content wise we were untouchable. Signal strength was complete garbage. After five years it was sold to ABC Disney, renamed, and watered down.

I held out for a year before I signed on to cohost the morning show at this new alternative rock station that had dropped a house on REV105 to stand out with the shift in musical trends happening in the late '90s to early aughts. Think Limp Durst and the start of Cookie Monster rock.

The new station I was working for positioned themselves as "Classic Alternative," whatever the shit that is. If it had been Pixies, the Waterboys, and Sonic Youth, that would've been dandy. Instead, it shoehorned bands like Spandau Ballet, Goo Goo Dolls, and Bronski Beat into an unlistenable mess.

Within our building the company also owned a classic rock station and a more metal-leaning station. Our sad piano-tie station was housed in the basement of the building and smelled like a diaper. My friend and cohost, Brian, and I would trudge upstairs for a smoke break and pass by the new metal station where stunts had women bobbing for dildos in the toilet to win tickets to see Jackyl. We would return to the aquatic studio to interview Winona LaDuke.

After a few years our weak format flipped to dentist office jams, and we were all let go. "Thanks for all of your hard work and dedication, who needs a box?"

In November 2004, I went in to interview for a new job. MN Public Radio was launching a new music station filled with hopes and promises. I'd done years of commercial radio, and as Liam Gallagher says, "Not for me, mate."

I sat in a conference room with three powerful hiring types who asked, "Why do you want to work at Public Radio?" I told them I wanted the opportunity to fail.

They looked at me like I'd kicked a kitten through an electric fence. Digging further into my awkward hole I spoke of needing the luxury to flop, because only real creativity is possible when the probability of failure is in place. I got the job, but to this day I don't truly know if they understood what I meant.

WORKING AT a radio station is never what people might assume it to be. First, you step off the elevator and you're immediately struck by silence. No music whatsoever. Even colleagues chatting around cube farms is about as raucous as the commentators for the Golf Channel.

Michael Ian Black, when he appeared on the morning show, summed it up best when he was led through the doors and astutely asked, "Is this a rock radio station? All I see is spreadsheets and sadness." Believe me, we got lots of mileage out of that, muttering under our breath that it should be the new station slogan.

This place took their donors as seriously as a heart attack, and the possibility of offending one of the check writers was like walking through a minefield.

I did a daily live newscast with my reporter friend Bob from the company's newsroom. We had wicked chemistry. He was more a social anthropologist than a traditional news guy, and we both loved reading obituaries on-air written by family members that pulled no punches. "Uncle Bill would give you the shirt off his back, if he ever wore one."

One newscast Bob reported about a mother gorilla at the zoo who had lost her newborn baby and held it in her arms for days. Christ on a cracker, that's utterly heartbreaking. Wrapping the story up I mustered a bleak "Well, I guess the good news is one less gorilla in captivity."

You would've thought I had made a joke about Al-Qaeda. Immediately I was informed that I would need to offer an on-air apology to the zoo and write a letter. One thing working for Public Radio is it made all of us great dancers. Dance this mess around any political leaning, any real opinions about world affairs. Our music station was held to the same standards of neutrality as the newsroom. When Agent Orange was elected in 2016, it nearly killed me.

THE MIX of two vastly different formatted stations sharing a floor and cube farm was always ripe for laughs. After seventeen years our station, which played a mix of new and vintage rock and roll, was still referred to within the company as "The Third Service." Think Gilligan's Island, "And the rest!"

First News, then Classical, then us the weirdos who came to work hungover and regularly hosted unbathed bands fresh off the tour bus into that expensive recording studio that had been donated by some dead rich codger. Who, might I add, would be spinning in their grave if they had seen Meshell Ndegeocello rolling joints on the gifted Steinway.

Lots of small edit suites were sprinkled throughout our floor, and many interviews with non–band types occurred in those rooms. Roving employees would crane their necks to get a view of who the day's guest might be. One interview I was thrilled to do was with Temple Grandin, the brilliant animal scientist, inventor, and autism educator.

She was incredibly sensitive to sound, light, and sudden movement. I was asked not to shake her hand upon greeting her. This woman is a true hero of mine and maybe my only guest to wear an authentic Nudie suit. We discussed her latest book and groundbreaking methods of the "Squeeze Machine" used in slaughterhouses, and then all of a sudden the fire alarm went off in the building. It was not only the most deafening high-pitched wail but was accompanied by strobe light warnings.

I nearly died at the thought of what this was doing to her. I was trying to be so sensitive to her needs that prior to her arrival I had removed all my jewelry anticipating any distraction. Now we were suddenly in a rave tent with the Chemical Brothers circa 1998. One of the most creative minds I'd ever met had to be quickly shuffled out the studio mid-interview.

Life in a cube farm ensures that you'll know the most details of at least four people by proxy. My "brand" was lost on many people, including one guy who I worked five feet from, who came to work dressed in a suit and tie one day, so naturally I asked him if he had a court date. He dryly handed my ass to me with, "No. I'm singing at my church after work." He looked upon me as Anton LaVey from that day on.

One of my favorite hosts on the classical station, who holds a special place in my heart, was a seasoned radio vet who regularly choked on crackers at her desk and carried a transistor radio with her listening to her live show. It was always a bit unnerving trying to insert a tampon in the bathroom stall when she would enter with Wagner blasting. There was a curious designated space with a door and a small couch and we never formally knew its purpose; we referred to it as the Divorce Room, the Biopsy Results Cubby, or simply the Cry Closet.

Manager offices lined the periphery, all with paper-thin walls so you could hear every phone call made or, even worse, you could audibly discern the program director, Potsy, disparaging one of us personally. I guess the reason we cogs never mentioned the lack of soundproofing was it was helpful to know which one of us he was currently throwing under the bus to upper management.

He was a career radio dude who spoke of the glory days of commercial alternative radio. Sorry to say, this guy never had a chance with me. He had managed to convince upper management he was Bono by attending company meetings with a predictable rock T-shirt under a suit coat. He had come from a big commercial alternative station where he was the afternoon drive host and never missed an opportunity to remind me that "he was the Mary Lucia of his former station." If you know of any appropriate response other than extreme discomfort, please let me know.

For whatever reason, the breaking news of a musician's croaking seemed to regularly occur five minutes before my show, forcing me to sit shiva for four hours illuminating their career and contributions. With some of my favorite artists the pain I felt was like I'd lost a friend: Tom Petty, Aretha Franklin, Justin Townes Earle, Prince, Charlie Watts, Kim Shattuck, Chuck Berry, Mark Linkous.

On many of these sad occasions, Potsy had the nerve to ask me if I needed him to jump on air with me, seeing as he clearly knew so much more about music than I did. Plus, I was "so good at the emotional part."

The death that had the most profound effect on me was David Bowie.

That morning, I was at home drinking coffee when my phone blew up. I received the news that my favorite artist of all time had died, and I got a text from work telling me to come in immediately. No time to process, no time for tears. Get in here and do your job. On the drive into work, I was listening to my friend who held the midmorning spot trying to soak in the words "David Bowie has died." Bowie was an artist that so many of us felt was our guy. Our favorite. You can geek out on a Bowie rant with friends for hours. Everybody loving a particular phase of his shape-shifting career and happy to tell you why. The incredible part is that no one is wrong.

I began to think of how grateful I was to have been on the same planet with someone of his talent. I got to see him perform live three times. He was no longer on the planet. Some would argue, was he ever? The very embodiment of fearless creativity. This was different. Things looked gray. My hero is gone. Yesterday while I was painting my toenails he was here. He would now be referred to in the past tense.

I am not a competitive music fan. I may know a fuck ton about him, but there will always be someone better versed. It wasn't a secret that I did obsessively adore his music. I think I played a tune almost every day on air. Now I had to put on my professional work dunce cap and report with a certain amount of objectivity. Then I thought, why do I have to be removed? I could never pretend to be. After all, this was the time people wanted to be together listening to this massive body of work. Screw objectivity. Let's grieve together.

There were television news crews at the station ready to capture a taste of what it was like working at a music station whose foundation was built on this man's music. What did we have to say? Luckily the shock of the news didn't cloud programming judgment. We would play all Bowie all day and night. When someone at this height of fame and meaning dies, people's natural instinct is to gather at a spot that represented their work and life. In Minneapolis, where would people pilgrimage? Around their radio of course.

I had friends who called in sick to work that day. I even know a musician whose birthday was on the day of his passing, and who was such a great fan they changed the day of their birthday.

Every cliché is real. You feel this loss on a personal level. I was in shock and disbelief to the point that I almost threw up in the parking garage. I was a wreck. How could I make anyone feel less devastated?

Listening to the entirety of his creative output communally is what will get us through this sad day. We'll talk about how much we love his music and style together. Everything is important. Your pain is my pain. The meaning of his songs will stay with us forever. All of us strangers who've never met share this in common. Today we are all friends. On the loneliest of days today, you are not alone. You may not remember everything that was said, but you'll never forget how it made you feel.

2
RAW MEAT

THE COMPANY'S MAILROOM WAS IN THE KITCHEN. WE ALL HAD SLOTS that were usually filled with band demos or junk mail.

One morning a colleague informed me I had mail that "smelled" like it needed my urgent attention. Smelled? By the way she said it I knew it wasn't going to be a bundle of Stargazer lilies.

Laying on the counter was a package wrapped in white butcher paper with my name on it. The contents were ten pounds of raw meat. A small crowd had gathered either by curiosity or the rank smell of dead flesh. This was my introduction to the Shit Bag who would turn the next few years of my life upside down.

Having to carry this package down the stairs and into the office of our HR department was humiliating. I knew in my gut this was different and more sinister than any unwanted attention from a fan I'd ever gotten. Suddenly, cig butts and a military dog tag seemed quaint.

Walking into someone's office with raw meat attracts the kind of response you'd expect. What the Actual Fuck is that?

I can laugh about it now when I think of the number of people who asked, "Who is it from?" As if it was a perfectly normal thing to receive in your work mail slot. There wasn't a return address written on the butcher paper, which also means it had to be dropped off in person at the station.

I went down to the lobby desk and asked the person on duty playing Candy Crush on their phone if they got a look at anyone dropping off this package for me. They didn't recall. Great. Sorry to bother you. Not much you can do without lobby cameras or any other means of identifying the hand deliverer of a ten-pound sirloin bouquet.

Letters in the mail at work were the next step in this nightmare. Never a return address and never a full name signature or even initials.

How could I even assume these were written by the raw meat creep? For starters, the tone of these letters and cards was ominous and unsettling. Sympathy cards, the kind you would send after a death in the family, with religious imagery. The presumed sense of overfamiliarity in what he wrote bothered me and felt incredibly manipulative. Many were typed, not handwritten.

A theme became clear almost instantly: the message he wanted to get across was I was in deep trouble, and he would be the only person that could help me. I had to start saving these letters as evidence.

After the raw meat there would be occasional packages or padded envelopes, the first few I opened before I begged the front desk to stop all packages from being brought up to the fourth floor.

One included a blurry polaroid photo of a man wearing a Halloween-type mask that covered their entire head. Some religious artifacts and dollar store nonsensical items. Several greeting cards signed off with the wildly inappropriate salutation: "I love you."

As frightening as all of this was, my mind never went further into the darkness of where this could escalate. It was contained at my job. I told a few friends at work. There just didn't seem to be any action I could take.

Then another sympathy card arrived, this time telling me that it would be terrible if anything ever happened to my dogs, say, poisoned or kidnapped. He would be the only one to understand and be there for me. That's when I thought my knees would buckle at my desk. There had been threatening tones in previous letters, but it was more that I was in deep trouble due inexplicably to my own life choices. For example, that I wasn't married.

At this point in my life, I was lucky enough to be a mom to two new Pugs. Now you're talking about my dog's safety, and buddy, you've lit the wrong match with me. I made an appointment to see a lawyer that worked for the company and gave her all the collected evidence over months. Any idiot could see that the handwritten ones were from the same person.

Without a name and return address I was without recourse.

I started to get the distinct feeling that people's attitude toward this unwanted attention was somehow due to my perceived kooky unconventional personality. "Only you, Looch" was uttered more than once.

Maybe before the term *gaslighting* became part of our current vernacular, this was my first real taste in no uncertain terms: you invite these weirdos, somehow this kind of shit only happens to you. This is your fault.

I couldn't possibly know then that this would be a constant battle I would fight with police officers, the courts, lawyers, and saddest of all, my own family members. Instinctively, I knew I had to be my own advocate. There was no meaningful understanding or conversation from management that wasn't couched with, "I've never dealt with this before, so uhh . . . I have no idea what to do." No shit you don't know what to do! You don't get it. It's happening to me and I'm telling you exactly how this is making me feel. Helpless, powerless, unsure of my own safety. But by all means I'll suck it up and be sure to forward-promote that upcoming interview with Jeff The Brotherhood. God forbid this should bleed into my work on air.

It became clear that I must also be my own detective. One day I was rummaging in a desk drawer at work, looking to see if perhaps he had sent something before the raw meat that I had overlooked and discarded into a junk pile. Jackpot! An unopened sympathy card addressed to me and signed with his initials from many months ago. I went into all my work email's deleted items, spam, trash, searching for anything from someone bearing his initials. The first email that matched his initials was from the man who had messaged me a year prior about how he'd lost his dog and was having such difficulty dealing with it. Bingo!

You dishonest creep. This was your sick way in.

I grabbed the envelope and ran down the stairs to our legal department offices. At the very least I had his name. The company's lawyer said she would put our digital team on high alert and sort through past emails to link him to more contact with me.

The company lawyer messaged me that she, as the legal rep of the radio station, had crafted a cease-and-desist letter sent to him. I asked if I could read what she wrote. She turned her laptop around for me to see. Written in a polite legalese manner, it was a request to kindly refrain from sending gifts to hosts. (Yes, she used the word GIFTS!) Then there it was in black and white, the courteous sign-off: "Thanks for listening to the station and supporting public radio." If I had been able to eat anything that morning it would've been projectile-vomited onto her law diploma hanging on the wall.

OVER THE MANY YEARS of being on the radio I've had my share of creepers. During the earliest days of my career I hosted a live radio show from a piano bar every Tuesday night, and there was a regular kook who started delivering unwanted pizzas to me during the show. I handled it in a way that seems so benign: I simply told him it was frowned upon to bring outside food into a restaurant. Not once mentioning that the very act of him continuously doing this skeeved me out.

There was another "fan" who regularly left notes on the windshield of my car where I parked in a ramp. Walking to my piece of shit Volvo at midnight after work and seeing something stuffed under a wiper blade made me ill and immediately ten times more aware of my surroundings.

Looking back, I don't know if it was my age and lack of experience or if the times were so different (I hate that expression for the record) that everyone around me, including myself, treated these unwanted gestures as completely docile and at worst a nuisance.

Years later one man in particular had been a barnacle of stress on me. It started with written letters and emails that progressively got more sexually explicit. His return address was St. Peter State Hospital for the criminally insane. Oh goody! His letters got more far out, with suggestions that I come down to visit him on a day pass and check him out for the day like a perverted library book. His planned activities for our date included visiting his aging mother and going to the local pawn shop. I finally called the hospital administration to see if they could put a stop to his disturbing correspondence.

Curiosity and a quick google search of his name provided me with more background than I wanted to know. He had stabbed a waitress he had been stalking on the West Bank in Minneapolis. He had been inside this facility for years. His parole came up every six months before a medical board to revisit his case and make the judgment if he was mentally fit to have visitors or day passes and other freedoms.

I felt like Yoko Ono, who I understand had to write yearly letters to Mark Chapman's prison begging them not to release him back into society. Twice a year I do the same. Unwanted invasive attention has always made me feel vulnerable. The notion that "You're in the public eye, and isn't this just a hazard of the job?" is the laziest misnomer and a theme I would have to dispel for years to come.

Receiving fan mail for a job like mine isn't uncommon. Sometimes it's a quick "thanks" email; other times someone licks a stamp and puts their thoughts into a mailbox. I've always been appreciative of anyone who would take the time to reach out about a story I told or to share a radio experience that falls under the right time, right song category.

One Monday morning I checked my desk phone voicemail and there were thirty-seven messages. All from the same dude. He was accusing me of wiretapping his phone, which I had apparently been doing for years. Naturally, he needed me to stop and leave *him* alone.

I asked Building Operations if it was possible to remove my phone number from the staff menu and to literally remove the phone from my desk. For the remainder of my time at the station I was unreachable by phone.

I used to chuckle when management needed a training course finished by a certain date. Their threat was always, If it's not completed, we'll cut off your email. Geez, promise?

3

DETOXICATED

My pattern of self-destructive behavior has historically been heightened by a traumatic event. I can easily transition into the most reckless fool in a nano. You know the drill if two glasses of red wine take the edge off, then a daily bottle of wine with a couple Vicodin might get me halfway to normal. My biggest downfall is how high functioning I can be while ripped.

I could take a handful of downers and be able to drive a school bus of kindergartners, no problem. I might be the only person to have assembled an IKEA bookshelf on Dilaudid.

My drug buddy and dear friend at the time, who is now a substance abuse counselor, hopped on the sad bastard train with me that summer to consume pills like Keith Moon and Judy Garland's love child. We had a dealer, we had code language, we had deep conversations, laughs, we threw up in people's yards. Tequila!

While attending an Oasis show at Target Center I had shoved a handful of Ativan into my hole, washed down with whatever booze was handed to me. The show was great. So I heard.

Upon learning that after their show the band had crossed the street to First Avenue to hang out, it made perfect sense that my party continue along with the single worst choice a person can make when drunk, and that is bar-close shots.

If you think you're a connoisseur of what you drink casually:

when blackout wrecked, your standard plummets to cheap champagne and paint remover.

My pals and I stumbled into the club, and dog knows why I headed straight for the off-limits DJ booth. Spotting Liam Gallagher in this VIP section it seemed the perfect time to not only meet him but to grill him about why they took Ryan Adams on tour as their opener.

How many times have I had a random drunk in my face wanting to discuss the finer points of music with unsteady legs, blowing flammable breath in my ear, bolstered with liquid courage to challenge me while punctuating every sloppy point with an obnoxious grab of my elbow?

Now here I was with someone I greatly admired, assaulting him with my question, "Don't you think Ryan Adams is a FRAUD?"

"A frog?" he responded in that heavy Manchester accent over the din of the live music.

"FRAUD!" I yelled louder, which made him laugh.

Next thing I knew we were smashing faces. I am dying of embarrassment in present time as I recount this.

Naturally, after a quick make-out sesh with Patsy Kensit's ex-husband, it only makes sense I would suddenly flee the scene of the crime and promptly take a header down the huge main stairs. Finding my friend, we linked arms to hold each other upright into the cold night air, emerging outside the club, where I proceeded to try and get into several cars idling for the traffic light to change.

I have zero recollection of what sober saint eventually drove me home, opened my apartment door for me, and left me in my coat sitting on the couch with the advice to drink water.

Waiting for my comeuppance was blissfully short as I spent the night on the bathroom tile.

Funnily enough it was the only time I ever had to call in sick to work with a hangover.

I also had to call the club's manager and apologize profusely for my idiot behavior. I begged her to pretend she had seen nothing and never talk about it with anyone. Maybe nobody saw me and my stuntman-like moves careening down the staircase after snogging a pop star. I would deny it was me if it ever came up.

The next day as if on cue I received an email from a local photographer with the subject line "I have some photos you might like to see." Sweet tap-dancing Jesus, not only had I been recognized but also photographed in my most cringy of public antics.

Lucky for me I knew the photographer, a friend. No blackmail. Just a reality check that you are not invisible at your most boorish.

It didn't take but a day to laugh at the images he captured. In fact, one is hanging by a fridge magnet in my home today.

THE STALKER had seemingly taken a temporary break, and I'll bet you that the station attributed his scarcity to that "threatening" letter sent by legal, which also managed to thank him profusely for his dedicated listening.

I had started hosting a specialty radio show on Friday nights, nothing but big loud guitar rock. Commence the renewed onslaught of letters. Now every song choice was sending hidden messages to him confirming my feelings for him. The tone of these letters started getting more suggestive sexually. Hostile, presumptive, and disapproving of my blatant promiscuity.

"When you have me why do you need to be a slut? Could you do your show while I'm fingering you?"

I felt completely violated. Now I had to overthink every song choice I put in my playlist. Could this tune be interpreted wrong? Most rock and roll songs are about shagging. All the fun of this show had instantly been replaced with paranoia on my part, trying to think like a sociopath.

I began to bow out of my life and shut down. It didn't feel like I was living my life as I knew it.

I had better start distancing myself from everything.

I got good at it. Too good at it.

FEELING DISCONNECTED from everyone in my life my next course of action still shocks me. I got a message on Facebook from an old friend I hadn't seen since we were teenagers. I remember him being pretty cool and I thought, what the hell, it might be fun to catch up. If nothing else, to leave my house.

We planned to meet for coffee at a neighborhood place. I wasn't sure I would even recognize him as his profile picture was of a plant.

A dude with thinning pinkish hair and sunglasses approached me and my immediate uh-oh radar went off. Sometimes a person's face tells their story before they utter a word. He looked like he'd been through some hard times.

We'd only made a bit of chat when we realized the coffee shop was nearing its 8 p.m. closing time. My first thought was relief: I can leave before we get further into this awkward reunion.

He mentioned that his apartment was literally around the corner and that we could continue "catching up" there. What possessed me to say "Sure" was either out of politeness or some morbid interest in what this guy's life had become the past twenty years. We traipsed across the street, and I followed him into the building, and we took the stairs to his apartment.

I kid you not, upon the door opening I was hit with an indescribable stench. It was like a freshly exhumed tomb. There were some awkwardly placed odds and ends of furniture scattered around, and I took a seat on an out-of-place office chair.

Catching up with an old acquaintance usually includes stories of work or relationships. The story he sincerely launched into had me eyeballing the nearest escape route.

I was still trying desperately to identify the smell that permeated his place when he proceeded to tell me of the current love affair he was having with his two internal parasites, which were named Crystal and Sparkle. His father as I had recalled held a prominent position as a physician at the university. He explained how his family didn't understand why he refused medical treatment as if he were discussing parental disapproval of someone's politics or religion.

I ask questions for a living interviewing bands on the regular. My motto has always been "Stay curious," so I had a few inquiries for death-stench boy. Trying to frame them as delicately as I could:

When did you meet your parasites and what exactly is so lovable about them?

He had answers, baby. According to him he was hosting some real honeys in his intestines. In my head I was trying to correlate the smell of his apartment with the story of his relationship(s).

Ruling out jumping out his third-floor window, I tried my best to treat this all as a normal interaction anyone could be having and made my excuse for having to leave. When I got home, I saw that he had messaged me saying it was great to catch up and he hoped he hadn't freaked me out.

All I could think of were the words of Chef in Apocalypse Now. "Never get out of the boat. Never get out of the boat."

4
UNTESTED MONKEY TRANQUILIZERS

I'LL PREFACE THIS NEXT CHAPTER BY EXPLAINING THAT I GREW UP IN a household that cherished NOTHING.

For example, there wasn't a lick of tradition when it came to Christmas in my family.

The holiday felt like a looming colonoscopy appointment; acquiring and decorating a tree nearly always ended in a flurry of profanity and hangovers.

No heirloom ornaments were carefully stowed in a safe place. Nobody was reaching into the sacred storage box while telling a delightful story of its fifty-year-old origin and heartfelt attachment to our dead Nana. A quicky trip to Walgreens to buy whatever generic red balls were left seemed more our style.

I may be exaggerating slightly, but I also seem to recall chucking fully decorated trees with lights in the alley on January 1.

WHEN I WAS VERY YOUNG, I can remember Christmas cards being sent to the house, and when I asked why in return we didn't send out holiday greeting cards, I was met with the non sequitur, "That's their problem." Okay. Wait, what? It makes as much sense now as it did then. No surprise those cards we got whittled down to maybe one or two a year, and they were usually sent by clueless out-of-state relatives who didn't regard us as a pack of wild animals or perhaps by the used car dealership that someone had visited in the past year.

There is so little physical documentation of my growing up, perhaps it's allowed me to create my own version of history and take some creative license. There may have been two photo albums in the house, but they stopped being supplemented sometime around 1969. We could assemble a better representation of a family photo album with mug shots and courtroom sketches than we could with actual Kodak moments.

Photos with shopping mall Santas or Easter Bunnies? Negatory.

Let me illuminate my family's level of investment in my childhood more clearly. One July afternoon my pops randomly asked me if I had graduated high school.

You get where I'm going?

No cute refrigerator drawings or book reports were saved. Keepsakes were referred to as clutter. The annual television viewing of *The Wizard of Oz* was dismissed as "that fantasy crap." On show-and-tell day when we had to bring in a treasured item from an older family member, I watched my classmates presenting Ellis Island entry papers from great-great-grandparents. Black-and-white beehive hairdo wedding portraits and tattered prayer cards.

I brought in Mott the Hoople's album *All the Young Dudes.*

Are you still with me?

When I was getting a passport for the first time, I asked my mom for my birth certificate and she casually explained it was probably thrown away during a move. Misplaced I get. Tossed out in a hefty bag? What the shit is that?

Being a lover of documentary films, I can say with confidence one could not be properly assembled about my family without actor reenactments or added animation.

That said, the voice-over narration would be, "Fire! HEYO!"

I see my adult friends whose families have kept boxes of sentimental items, silly nothing Mother's Day cards, baby booties, home movies, locks of freaking hair?

The archaeology of love. Time capsules of laughs and feeling deeply connected. I am genuinely happy for those lucky enough to have someone act as the protector of their young life and memories.

So here I am today. A big honking weirdo of contradiction.

I live for vintage clothes, architecture, and furniture—absolutely obsessed with the imagined romance of something created seventy-five years ago made to stand time.

Then there's the side of me that doesn't want to eat leftovers and has no interest in listening to recorded live albums. If I was there the first time it happened, I think I got the gist. I find no need to revisit. Which makes sense having parents busy destroying documentation of my birth record and questioning if I was a high school graduate when I was in my first year of college.

I WOULD NEVER CALL my childhood traditional. Typical latchkey kid. Both parents working wasn't unusual in our neighborhood.

ML worked in a bank; Hal worked for Cadillac. Please note that we didn't call them Mom and Dad. Their first names sufficed with the bonus of eliminating any traditional expectations of parental structure.

Punishment never took the form of being ordered to my room because that was my haven. Real retribution was being told to stay down here in the living room with your family. My idea of utopia was bringing our Collie dog, Pansy, into my room where I would sit in my closet and read to her. I had a thing for hanging out in closets. Our house was quite old and had some rad outdated features. A maid's buzzer in the dining room floor, a carriage door on the front porch, a dumb waiter, clothes chutes, a bomb shelter, and random crazy closets.

The cedar closet smelled divine, where clothes hung in dry-cleaning plastic. Or my favorite weird closet, situated in the wall above your head. Laying down it was about the size of a coffin. I would beg to sleep in there instead of my bed.

Growing up with rampant addiction in your family is a mess. Especially when you see drunken-fool behavior actually lauded and singled out as a strong character trait. If you're the addict who can hold a job, hold an audience, and bring humor or color into every room you enter, then the disease of addiction takes a back seat to these whimsical talents. To quote Dudley Moore, *yes,* Dudley Moore: "Everyone who drinks is not a poet. Maybe some of us drink because we're not poets."

As a kid I tried to let so much disappointment slide, forever careful to take my personal feelings out of someone else's poor choices and lifelong addictions. More than once reminded I should be grateful Hal never drunkenly put anyone's head through a wall. That's right, this is how low the expectations of parenting went.

Having such an age gap between my siblings probably didn't help me understand any of this. As witness to all the drugging and drinking as a kid being years away from my own first taste and battle, my reactions were purely emotional and not that of a mature thinker. You see their protecting the drink over you as a choice.

Damn straight I took it personally. Foolish attempts to hide booze from Hal or dilute half-drunk vodka bottles with water is still a memory that goes right to the most tender part of little Mary. Sitting at a dinner table with my adult family getting hammered felt unsafe, and more importantly to a kid, I felt excluded.

When I was eight, I had a sleepover at a neighbor's house, which felt exciting to me: I always felt special to hang out with the older girls. We had decided to camp out in sleeping bags on the living room floor. The father of this household was a wicked alcoholic/health nut (?) who listened to Hank Williams on a reel to reel. He was never out of his work uniform and would slide across their wood floors in moccasins that he didn't actually put on his feet but rather smashed his heel into the slipper.

There had been uncomfortable situations I had experienced at the friend's house that in my child's mind were assigned to "He's just a big weirdo." His "playfully" scratching at the closed bathroom door when I was using it. Trying to grab my towel off me after a run through the sprinkler.

Their dining room table was the center for Play-Doh and coloring books. His sitting uncomfortably close, staring at me intently while drawing me as I sat there coloring, felt strange and I didn't like it, but what could I do? I was happy to be invited over to an older girl's house. He had a designated chair in the living room and an ever-present case of Old Milwaukee bottled beer next to it. I was a light sleeper even as a child, so naturally I was awakened by the sudden loud sound of the television set. I opened my eyes and in the blue cast from the tube saw my friend's dad seated in his chair, bottle in hand, still wearing his mechanic's uniform looking at me. I was confused. This is a kid's sleepover: why are you watching TV at 2:30 in the morning? I closed my eyes and pretended to be asleep not knowing exactly what to do.

The next sound I heard to my horror was the unzipping of my sleeping bag and the musty stink of boozy breath next to me. Why was I the only one awake for all of this? I bolted upright and half-hopped out of the sleeping bag and announced, "I have to go home!" I grabbed my clothes and in my pajamas went to their front door completely confused that he was following right behind me. Barefoot I walked the half a block home while he trailed a couple of feet behind me.

I didn't have a key to my house, nor did I plan to be walking home at 3 a.m., so I had to knock loudly on our front door. It's a miracle anyone heard me. My mom answered, naturally confused to see me standing in the porch light dressed in my pj's. She looked past me to see that I had been safely chaperoned home by the drunken predator and even gave him a friendly wave of thanks.

What has predictably stayed with me was ML's lack of outrage or even inquisition as to what led up to my fleeing a sleepover in the middle of the night.

For what it's worth, I told ML exactly what happened.

We never talked about it again.

It's taken years for me to accept that ML had limitations on what she could and could not give me. Her mother stuffed her own daughter's sexual abuse aside as a child and maybe unintentionally assigned some shame to it. Clearly, she too fell short in what she could give as well.

This story sadly doesn't make me unique, and it's caused me low-grade shame for all my life. I know people who were sexually assaulted and far worse, including my mom.

This isn't a trauma contest, just a part of my story.

Having struggled with anxiety and depression my entire adult life, I had been seeing a shrink off and on for years, unraveling the usual wealth of material that comes from having parented myself. You should know that declaring a lifelong struggle with depression and anxiety is nothing exceptional to me. I'm not special in this regard. I don't think I know anyone who hasn't dealt with both.

Hereditary? Baked in? Environmental? Situational? Yes, to all of it.

The shrink I had been seeing was highly intelligent and spoke like Ben Stein. Bueller? Bueller? He represented a strong father figure with his sensible suggestions and furrowed-brow-style listening.

He must've had stake in certain Pharmaceutical Companies because his desk drawer was brimming with the latest antidepressants. The in-person sessions had been weaned to him merely writing me prescriptions. For all I knew they were untested monkey tranquilizers that he had in his desk.

I got lazy and stopped researching each individual drug prescribed and found myself not only self-medicating but also popping whatever free sample he had on hand. Some of these were doozies.

Most people when under such duress would up the self-medicating; me, however, I decided this is the perfect time to get clean and stop taking absolutely everything. Detoxing alone at home, telling no one about it.

God only knows what reason I was taking the antipsychotic medication Zyprexa for depression/anxiety. The former shrink with access to the drawer of meds had prescribed them to me more than two years earlier. I hadn't been in for a med check in about as long.

I was also on Prozac, Klonopin, Restoril, Gabapentin, and Xanax.

My self-medicating included a daily bottle of red wine, Vicodin, Oxy-anything I could get my hands on. The lowest of lows was dipping into a distant friend's meds who was dying of cancer.

When the stalking ramped up, turning my guts inside out, it would be safe to assume that for most people a traumatic time in one's life might also be the moment the self-medicating goes into action.

Me? No. I stopped everything cold turkey and I didn't tell anyone. It sounds almost masochistic as if I wanted to feel the pain more deeply with no interference.

I've always been a relatively responsible addict, you could say. I took a week of vacation from work to withdraw at home.

So we're all on the same rotten page: I quit everything. Prescribed. Recreational. A serious alcohol dependency, and in the interest of my poorly crafted plan I started smoking cigs again.

I'm not sure there is a new way to describe detoxing from opioids. Pretty much every person's withdrawal includes extreme chills, shakes, nausea, the feeling that your skin is crawling, and no sleep. I'm talking almost three days of sleepless writhing. How many times did I reconsider what I was doing? Absence of sleep compounding the physical sickness is about the time you feel like you are losing your mind. And I was.

I stayed in my winter coat and shuffled from one piece of furniture to the other trying to bend my body into a shape that didn't hurt.

More than once I convinced myself that if I died, no big deal. I'd accomplished much, what else did I have to do? People live too long anyways. I was trying to intellectualize my demise while withdrawing from narcotics and alcohol. In that moment this made sense to me.

My best friend, Jess, had a key to my house. One afternoon while dry-heaving into the big bowl I used for popcorn, she let herself in, announcing from the start that it was she who was entering the house along with the kindest words I've ever heard: "Don't get up, I'm just here to clean your bathroom."

I don't know what's more remarkable, the fact that she did this on her own initiative or that I let her proceed to clean my vile bathroom.

To illustrate that we share a brain and are sisters of the soul: if I croaked today, she could complete this book and it would probably be better.

5

POSITIVITY, DO WE MARK YOU PRESENT, OR DO WE MARK YOU LATE?

Am I the only person alive who has adored Prince my entire life but wants him to remain a mystery?

I'll answer my own question: most likely I am alone. Nothing new there.

I was always the goon saying that I could never envision Prince doing average things like plunging a toilet, waiting for the cable guy, owning a pair of Crocs, trying to find which smoke-alarm battery is dead and beeping, stepping in cat barf, etc.

But dig, if you will, the picture . . .

Since his untimely passing, people far more eloquent than I have tried to sum up what he meant to all of us. Many have done a brilliant job in unraveling the mystique of his genius. What can I possibly add?

Normally, it is very much in my nature to dig deep into my heroes' stories and devour their written biographies like a rock and roll vulture. But Prince? Nope.

Ironically, my lack of interest in knowing all the details is a mystery in itself. Being such a loyal admirer for so many years, on the day

Prince died I felt genuinely disoriented every time I tried to speak. This whole town felt different to me, it felt stripped of its identity and light, and maybe with that, a bit of my own identity was missing as well. My shine was dulled down so dim I felt like a faintly illuminated X-ray.

Given the nature of his death, naturally the frenzy began to find out what all Prince's secrets were—what was he keeping from the public, as if he owed us any explanation: "I saw you on the *1999* tour; I DESERVE to know what you struggle with in your personal life."

Oh god, here we go, I braced myself.

Why did I get so indignant about people's quest to get to the bottom of Prince's accidental overdose? Buncha reasons I suppose. Most primitively, I feel very strongly that there needs to be a deeper level of understanding and mercy regarding addiction. Even in the words *pain* and *killer,* the pain frustratingly gets overshadowed by the noun *killer,* which I guess makes for a more readable headline. Yes, opioid addiction is very real and serious and can cut the life short of someone you want more from. Trust me: I wouldn't weigh in one single thought about this if I haven't myself had a shitty front-row seat. Reality is just a crutch for those who can't handle drugs, right? But crucial to be mindful of is that people who live in personal darkness can create some of the most vivid, meaningful, and colorful art.

My desire to only be up close and personal with Prince's music and not his private life surely explains why I have no interest to tour Paisley Park and absorb the staged personal objects that are meant to pull back the curtain and let us in on what he was all about.

The family have assured everyone that it was always Prince's desire to have Paisley Park turned into a museum, and I get how much it will mean to fans worldwide. I harbor no judgment. Everyone who wants to go should go and wear assless chaps!

Just sayin'—I won't be there.

Maybe because I think he was bigger than what can be contained behind a velvet rope with tour guides and a gift shop. In my mind, heart, and booty, Prince is infinite and free. His will always be my go-to favorite music, and some of the most memorable live performances I was ever lucky enough to witness in big and small venues will remain highlights of my life.

The wealth of quotable lyrics is staggering. I recall laughing for about seventeen straight days after overhearing a six-year-old girl at Cub Foods proclaiming, "Ooh yeah, ooh yeah / I wanna bust that body."

I know plenty of people who worked directly with Prince, and they all have stories of his unpredictability and his unsurpassed attention to detail and style. I've enjoyed hearing those stories to a voyeuristic degree, but I don't feel comfortable retelling them. They feel sacred. I even have my own Prince story, which I will never tell.

I know that part of the grieving process is to share your own Prince stories, to gather a feeling of connectedness. I do feel some people have really been able to express the power of Prince as an artist in funny, thoughtful stories. I will share one that perfectly describes his mastery as a performer: a known musician in town was watching Prince perform at First Avenue and said to his band buddy standing slack-jawed next to him, "I am embarrassed to be alive."

Prince's ability to confuse, challenge, and Ghett Off through a public career spanning his entire adult life while retaining that sense of mystery is something I marvel at and will always hold with so much respect. I am happy with what he gave me, and I am happy with what he did not give me. That is the part reserved for my imagination and dreams.

Something tells me Prince would've dug that picture.

MUCH MORE has come to light about Prince's accidental overdose.

How he obtained so many different prescriptions for highly addictive opiates. It isn't that I don't completely understand people wanting answers on both a personal and legal level. I do.

None of us knows exactly what was in Prince's heart and his daily thoughts; we can speculate, but it's not going to bring him back to life. Were the people supplying him with these pills out to hurt him?

I'm guessing not willfully. Being in the position of loving someone dependent on the perpetual numbing is agony in itself. Do we feel compassion for the "enabler"?

Usually, they are almost easier to blame than the person putting the drugs in their own mouth.

Have you ever known someone addicted to drugs, lived with one, been raised by one, or are you/have you been one yourself? Being addicted to drugs, to me, doesn't besmirch the character of a person's heart. Do addicts do horrible things? Of course. Do they hurt the people around them who sometimes love them the most? Absolutely.

Do I define Prince as a drug addict? Nope. It was a part of him. A part.

Self-destruction is never easy to comprehend unless you've been there and held the blade or bottle in your own hand. Addiction to painkillers is an ugly black hole. Most people start using because they are in physical pain. The downward spiral to chase the dragon is a harrowing ride. Somewhere along the way, that physical pain intertwines with emotional pain.

This is not meant to be a debate about tough love and whether it ultimately helps anyone into recovery. Should the addicted person be held accountable? Yes. Was Prince feeling and accepting accountability? I have no idea.

A little mercy and understanding are most needed when the person addicted is doing the most damage to their relationships and to themselves, or even more needed when they are gone. If you aren't capable of mustering up that kind of benevolent feeling toward the person using, then walk away if you can and know you did all that you could. You have to look after your own heart.

I just hope that we keep our souls open to those who struggle, and specifically with Prince, that we not let the sickness overshadow the creative gifts he bestowed upon us.

6

NOW WHAT HAVE I DONE?

WHAT I'M ABOUT TO TELL YOU I'VE TOLD ONLY ONE PERSON IN MY life. This might be the point at which you think I am the nutjob.

Over so many years I've had meaningful correspondences with listeners I've never met nor ever intended to. One such email pen pal was Davey. He was smart, hilarious, an amazing writer, and suicidal. It's tough to articulate how I knew in my core he was no threat to me. There was never a suggestion of meeting in person.

Quite the juxtaposition from a different stranger's communication with me.

This pen pal friendship was based on intuition. Nothing he wrote to me ever seemed out of bounds or inappropriate. He told me nothing I hadn't heard before or felt myself.

I tried to encourage him to write because his emails were perfectly written chapters of a life of struggle and humor. On par with Kurt Vonnegut. He shared with me his battle with agoraphobia, caring for his elderly mother. Living on disability. In complete contrast to Shit Bag's delusional letters, Davey was a compassionate deep thinker. We didn't exchange emails often, but when we did they felt natural. I felt honored he would lay himself bare to a stranger, never asking for anything in return.

One thing he and I had in common is we are both lifelong cutters. Discovering that was like sharing an astrological sign. What, wait, you're also a Leo?

How to explain being a lifelong cutter . . .

I imagine each individual has their own "reasoning" for this type of response to trauma/depression. For me it was controlled pain. Pain I could manage. Self-inflicted and specific. I would tend my own wounds (a fucked-up way to express self-care).

There is no logical way to explain self-harm in this form. I can only speak for myself. It has never been a haphazard act for me. Quite the opposite. I'm methodical and intentional when I cut.

A sharp double-edged razor dragged across my arm releases anger I cannot express with words. The anger isn't toward me, which might be the hardest part to digest. I know some people have suggested it's a way to feel when life has numbed you out.

I feel everything. It's about disciplined pain. If some stranger is intent on making my life hell, and seemingly there is nothing I can do to stop it, this is one thing I have power over.

When short-sleeve weather comes around, you're exposed. You either hide the scars or you don't. I didn't.

Procuring the razor blades is always a whole to-do. You must find the right drug store that sells the blade you prefer. Next you must buy bandages at a separate store. Casually walking up to the checkout counter with three packs of double-edged blades, band aids, and a copy of *In Touch Weekly* will arouse suspicion and stink eye.

It's a whole ritual.

Who knows? Maybe the staff at Walgreens don't pay much attention to your purchases. Just because I noticed what people were purchasing, I assumed so did the cashiers. I can't help but sneak a peek at others' curated baskets.

I remember one night standing in line at a twenty-four-hour grocery store behind a man buying three bottles of bleach. Meth lab or cleaning up a murder scene.

I UNDERSTAND DEPRESSION ON the level where you start searching for any reason to get out of bed. Through specific stories exchanged with Davey I could sense him increasingly leaning into those desperate thoughts.

I thought of my own life. I live alone, and I have intentionally isolated myself in the past year. I've been unable to speak about what has been happening to me.

I can accurately gauge my depression level by the amount of loose change on the floor of my apartment. Once there was a dime on my living room floor for seven months. Somehow the effort required to pick it up was too much.

Aside from a job, what gets me out of bed every morning on days when I feel that if I weren't here all this pain would be gone?

My dogs.

What I ended up doing is so frowned upon and even difficult to talk about now.

I bought Davey a dog.

I roughly knew where he lived and saw that there was an adoption day at his local PetSmart. I searched the website and saw a beautiful one-year-old Golden Retriever mix, and not thinking twice I sent the check. I emailed Davey to tell him to go to that adoption day and check out the Golden Mix Pup, and if he fell in love, it was his. Of course, he still had to fill out the necessary information and be vetted and approved. I was fully prepared to be the new owner of a Golden Retriever if things took a turn.

That Saturday Davey took Gibbs to his forever home. Now our correspondence was mostly about the renewed love and purpose he felt. Plenty of photos and beautiful stories of shared emotional support unlike anything he had ever known. They shared their lives together until Gibbs passed away last year at the age of fifteen. He had sent me a letter in the mail sharing the news. I bawled the entire drive home that evening. I unraveled a bit.

The focus of my initial intention came crashing down upon me. I surprised myself how shattered I felt for Davey's loss. Clearly there was a deeper level of importance I was trying to make sense of. Gibbs was his dog.

Gibbs was my attempt at rescuing a man I would never meet.

I know what a risk that was and still shudder when I think about how it could've been disastrous and how irresponsible of me to think I held the answer for a stranger.

I've let go of the shame I felt at how inappropriate my solution was sixteen years ago.

And now you know the secret thing I did.

7
Q AND A-HOLE

INTERVIEWING BANDS WAS MY FAVORITE PART OF THE JOB—A CHANCE to connect to a group of strangers in real time, not to mention the absurdity of this going out live on air. There is nothing natural about the process. You walk into a studio with four or five strangers, and you have to read the room immediately. Your hope is to engage on a level that is meaningful or amusing, which in turn connects these musicians to the listening audience.

If I was trying to compile a greatest hits of radio interviews I've done for a compilation reel, maybe I should include some of the worst as well. I can only imagine they might be just as interesting to a listener. You can hear the flop-sweat coming through your speakers. On second thought, it won't get me a job but I'll gladly share some with you.

Interviews of artists I personally love are especially challenging. It took me a long time to understand that it's not fair to expect that our conversations will translate into something as meaningful as I find their work.

There have been many I loved, where I learned something truly special—indelible lessons. Trent Reznor was a standout. His retelling of Johnny Cash, in the twilight of his huge career, covering one of his songs, was tremendous. Reznor described the feeling of scribbling the words to "Hurt" in a journal as a young, gothy man. Flash-forward many years, and he's hearing those words come back to him in Cash's sage baritone: "I hurt myself today to see if I'd still feel." He described it as one of the most humbling and powerful experiences in his career.

I was then compelled to venture into the uncertain waters of talking about David Bowie, as they shared both a working relationship and genuine friendship. Hearing him explain that Bowie was the only artist who exceeded any expectations he had, first as a fan and then a collaborator, reaffirmed what I already suspected as a Freak Out in a Moonage Daydream fan myself. My final question to him was if he thought David Bowie owned a pair of sweatpants. The answer, predictably, was NO.

I fondly remember my conversation with legendary writer, historian, actor, and Pulitzer Prize–winner Studs Terkel, who at the time of our interview was rounding 137 years of age. Despite the squealing feedback from his hearing aids, I was on the edge of my seat the entire time. This cat was a storyteller from another time. The fact that he could recount a detailed story of falling down a flight of stairs and breaking his neck with such humor and poetry had me laughing so hard I should've been struck by lightning on the spot.

Addressing his advanced years, he left me with this golden nugget: he told me that he would never have understood as a younger man that the most important part of growing older was the desire to feel needed. As my uncle would holler before sinking the eight ball in the corner pocket, "SCHOOL'S OUT!"

DURING THE PANDEMIC, my first Zoom interview was a transatlantic chat with Laura Marling. This was the infancy of the Covid era, so zero kinks had been worked out. A musician at home is not a sound engineer. The annoying sound lag/echo was a fresh hell challenge, which resulted in lots of talking over each other. Coupled with intermittently frozen video screens, I could not wait for it to be over. (No shade on Marling.) Thinking we had signed off, I declared to myself aloud, "WHAT THE FUCK WAS THAT!" Whoops, we were still connected. Probably the only clear thing she heard me say all interview.

I also despise phone interviews, known in the trade as "phoners." They always sound like a 911 call transcript.

While doing a phoner with Richard Hell, I asked if he believed in Revolution, which he mistakenly heard as Evolution, resulting in a few minutes of awkward miscommunication from the godfather of punk, his assumption being he was talking to some hayseed flat-earther.

I always prefer the in-person chat. One, I love to see what a person is wearing. Give me faces, footwear, and road funk. Two, it's a helpful visual to know if the guest wants to kick my ass, or the other way around.

I'm always impressed, when a band is performing a song that contains profanity, how some are able to substitute the choice word for something quite clever. Brother Ali is one of the best at radio-friendly, on-the-spot self-editing. Others hit a brick wall in this situation, and then I love when they need to have a serious discussion amongst themselves about what word to use instead of "shit."

When the legendary Charles Bradley was in studio the first time, he had a room full of musicians with him, maybe even a Dap-King or two. I asked Charles if he would like to introduce his band, and the look on his face was priceless: he looked around the studio and, as if for the first time, he realized there were other people playing with him. Naturally, he had no idea what their names were. This wasn't a pickup band for the night; I can only assume he had been traveling and playing with these dudes for quite some time. "Uh, that's the drummer, guitar player, et cetera," he tentatively offered. The band was sympathetic and laughed it off, understanding that if you're lucky enough to be shredding with the Screaming Eagle of Soul on stage night after night, he doesn't need to know your name.

Early on in The Current's tenure, Lou Barlow was coming in and we were informed beforehand he had requested that he would need vegan sausage and wine for the morning session. I don't think we actually provided him with tofu dogs, but I seem to remember someone scrambling for the hooch.

I had King Khan on live for a "chat" (I think I said eight words in total), and if you aren't familiar with his vibe, I have one word for you: cape. It was the most out-of-control fifteen minutes I've had in recent memory. It was like a hubcap rolling down a hill—no way was I going to catch up, so instead I just gave in and let it go. Not always pleasing for a program director, but for the fans of this stream-of-consciousness anarchy, it was quite a listen.

When Nick Lowe and Ian McLagan were scheduled to be on tour together, their first stop was Minneapolis, and it included a session at The Current. Minutes before the session, we had just received the unthinkable news that Ian was in the hospital struggling for his life. I was completely unhinged. I had to walk into a room to meet my idol for the first time and navigate around this sensitive situation. I shook Nick's hand, introducing myself almost in tears, and looked around me to fully absorb his backup band were Los Straitjackets, a group who perform wearing Mexican wrestling masks. Suddenly everything became so surreal as they stood huddled around sound checking and thoughtfully discussing the Ian predicament Nacho Libre style; it threw things into an absurd perspective.

Boss up and do your job, Looch.

I'm sure over the years you've heard interviews on The Current that were fantastic and revealing with spot-on musicianship. I'm just as certain you have listened to some frightfully awkward exchanges that made you as the listener want to rip your own arm off and beat someone with it. Take some comfort in knowing that the DJ floundering is just as aware of their publicly documented audio flop-sweat.

I was walking down a corridor for a live interview with alt-J, a band that seemed to me to be only taking up unnecessary space. Just before entering the studio, I was informed I could only direct my questions to one of them. A very Mariah Carey–like demand. It didn't help that I didn't know who the fuck was alt and who was J. I figured whichever poser didn't look at me was the diva in question. There's only two of them making this dreck, and I still have no idea which one I directed my questions to.

I nearly exchanged punches with a DJ duo from LA. Going into the interview, all I knew about them was that Joaquin Phoenix had directed one of their videos.

The lead douche never removed his sunglasses, yet I could feel his eyes boring a hole into me. I asked a fairly innocuous question that was either perceived as a slight or, frankly, I don't know what. He took a full thirty-second beat of silence, so I did what I always do in those situations, which is change the subject or insist another tune should be performed. Ray-Ban Bag of Anger had a real problem with that and accused me of being rude.

What happened next usually only happens in my dreams, but I said exactly what I was feeling out loud. "I don't care if you want to talk or not, I have a headache." I was wearing a short skirt that day, but I was fully prepared to go at him like a wild spider monkey.

The "interview" ended when one of them finally walked out in the middle of this excruciating cringe fest. My producer reassured me we wouldn't air it, to which I vehemently insisted we do air it exactly as is. I had to believe if I was sitting on an on-ramp in rush hour, hearing two strangers nearly coming to blows would be worth a sustaining membership.

Or, at the very least, they'd get to hear an engineer asking the offended guest what he was looking for, only to be told, "An exit."

You can't control rock and roll . . . and really, would you want to?

8

EATING OUT OF A PAIL

I'VE NEVER BEEN AVERSE TO CHANGE, BUT THE KINDS OF CHANGES that were happening to me I became resentful of.

Going out to a show was no longer an option. Not knowing who this stalker was or what he looked like—he could be anywhere. And if a mentally unstable person warns you time and again that he's watching you and knows where you are always, you believe it.

I now owned my first house and felt my independence as a woman. I had taken satisfaction in taking care of the yards front and back, even shoveling snow I saw as strength building.

Suddenly the act of having my back turned away from my house felt unsafe. I had to have my full attention on what was always in front and behind me.

Leaving work was a constant looking over my shoulder, checking the back seat of my car keys in hand to poke someone's eyes out. The second I got home I threw every lock and closed every blind.

I would be standing in my kitchen still in my winter coat and hat, fumbling to open a bottle of wine. This was the very first thing I did. Before feeding the critters even. Letting my dogs out became a concern. I would stay outside with them in the backyard until they finished they bidness, jumping every time the motion lights went off. Forget about walking them. That routine had been taken from us.

My social circle of friends was whittled down. I was isolating out of fear that no friend would want to hear about this violation that was consuming me.

It might be in my nature, for as big a dog lover as I am I can relate to the behavior of a cat.

I'm not feeling well, I'm going to hide. Dying alone under the basement stairs seems preferable to getting lots of attention and concern.

My on-air work changed as well; I was no longer comfortable revealing anything personal about myself. No longer could I tell listeners about an upcoming event I wanted to attend for fear that Shit Bag was listening. I felt I was getting more generic by the day.

A big deal in radio is broadcasting daily from the State Fair, which I had done for my entire career in radio. The fishbowl studio and people craning their necks to get a look at the voice they had been hearing for however many years.

Being the afternoon drive host, I was out there working Monday to Friday doing my radio show live in front of people wearing paper hats in the shape of a pickle sitting on benches hoovering down a pail of French fries. Yes, I said *pail*: if not familiar, many of the food options are served in a pail. Nobody is concerned with portion control.

THE STATE FAIR is a beloved end-of-summer tradition for many, but make no mistake—the freak-watching has always been just as important.

It had gotten to the point where I had to write a note inside the fishbowl not to make fun of passersby: a hot mic is always a possibility in live radio.

I did a daily live interview on the small stage we had next to the booth.

The Summer of 2014 during all this gut-churning anxiety, five days a week I had to get my ass on a city bus, transfer once, and do my show live from the fair. Did it bother me that I had to ask station management for security? Yes.

Security was arranged. However, the guy who was assigned to

watch out for me gave me the creeps. All he did was talk about firearms and how I should seriously consider owning a gun.

One sweltering afternoon a woman rushed the glass of our broadcast booth with something written on the palm of her hand in black Sharpie. Scrawled on her outstretched hand were the words "Softball Camp." I've never played softball in my life, so I awkwardly shrugged my shoulders and turned my back from her.

Later that afternoon I was talking to one of our digital social media employees and told him of the rando hand message. He asked what she looked like and clearly seemed uncomfortable. Apparently, she had shown up to the station's headquarters earlier looking for me, giving off red-flag vibes.

By this point the lobby security had tightened up enough that visitors had to show a driver's license for scanning. A few calls were made, and my digital pal Wells was able to ascertain she was the same troublesome tweeter they had been monitoring. This was all news to me. I already had Ted Nugent as a security guard, but protection was amped up because the following day's tweet from Softball Camp was, "Going to see Lucia, Lock 'n' Load."

That afternoon her scanned photo ID was passed around to the mostly senior citizen public radio volunteers, who bless their hearts were out there hawking Super Freak Garrison Keillor swag in exchange for free admission. It was hardly the SWAT team.

Scheduled for a live chat on stage that day was the chef Andrew Zimmern. I walked out onstage and started scanning the small crowd that had gathered to hear the infamous chef talk about exotic insects he had eaten. Apologies to Mr. Zimmern: all I could focus on was whether I was going to be shot before, during, or after he had time to plug his new book.

My friend Bob from the newsroom was out there that day volunteering at the booth and had been given a heads-up about this whack job.

No sooner had I introduced my guest when I saw Softball Camp sitting in the fourth row with her purse open on her lap; she was fishing around in it. I am not making this up. Bob and I exchanged a panicked look, and at that moment she bolted out of her seat with Bob chasing her into the crowd. He saw that she had a knife in her hand. She easily disappeared into a vast sea of double strollers and people carrying pails.

9
THERE GOES THE LAST DJ

THERE ARE COUNTLESS OLD STORIES ABOUT RADIO AIRPLAY AFFECTING a musician's suck-cess. You've heard 'em: "The DJ flipped over the disc to play the B-side, and TA-DA! You've got yourself a hit record."

The hitch in all these tales is that the radio DJ's autonomy was imperative in the process. Also, all these stories originated in the 1950s.

I've often fantasized about giving a TED Talk on the real-real lack of freedom any on-air host has in assembling a playlist in modern times. It would likely be super boring and sparsely attended, but it might clear up the age-old assumption that total freedom of choice lies within every radio DJ's grubby mitts.

The way in which music gets played on radio is a mathematical formulation—seemingly designed to eliminate the human element. This is nothing new. As long as someone is coughing up dough for advertisements, the leaner a playlist becomes. There are numerous metrics and statistics that make me go stupid.

The actual Time Spent Listening (TSL) is such a fleeting number of minutes. Program directors are always chasing after those fickle channel changers, which dictates frequency of spins in rotation. So when a loyal radio lover is listening all day at work, for example, they will hear repeat songs and artists. Then they email the radio DJ, irritated about the repetition. The truth is these songs are being played more frequently for the casual listener, not the hardcore eight-hour-a-day fans. So, to be clear, the DJ isn't picking these songs, but since we're on the front line, we take the bullet.

A certain amount of creative freedom sneaks in when a DJ is allowed to play a lesser-known tune—known in old-radio-hack verbiage as a "deep cut." Or—get ready to clutch those pearls—breaks the rules entirely and plays something they brought from home that is not already in the system. Guaranteed, no one on the music programming side relishes the rogue DJ.

Meet me. It is I, rogue DJ. The cilantro of radio.

I foolishly still believe music programming can be an art form, which necessitates the host to bend, break, and otherwise ignore the rules. If a person has a great ear and wide knowledge of music, there will always be an audience appreciation for deviant choices. That (admittedly more limited) audience has always been my chosen people.

Honesty has been frowned upon my entire career in the business of show. But for twenty-eight years, I subscribed to the philosophy that if I can't say something genuinely enthusiastic about a song, best to move on and talk about the thing you do love. The backhanded compliment I heard from management time and again was, "You're really interesting when you're talking about something you love." No guano. Saying nothing about a band says everything, I believe.

If I'm an authentic person on-air, people understand my personal taste and don't need to hear faux toadying over an artist or song that doesn't do it for me. I will admit that, on rare occasions, I have done the unthinkable and pulled the fader down midsong on a tune that was doing me great bodily harm. I'm sorry, Joanna Newsom. It was nothing business—it's strictly personal.

Scientific studies show music can elicit a physical response from someone in a deep vegetative state or soothe someone transitioning between life and death. That is a powerful notion.

I like to imagine myself hovering precariously somewhere between life and death and what song could be played to get me to rip out the tubes, rise from my deathbed, and lunge for the OFF button.

I DO LOVE LIVING in a world where everything is not for everyone. Perfection is a bore.

That doesn't mean I haven't given thought to a few helpful ideas to get us closer to a better planet.

Laughing gas would be included with every on-hold call to your bank, phone provider, government office, or cable network.

Izzy Stradlin would've emerged and been acknowledged by everyone as the most talented member of Guns N' Roses.

You could teach your dog to vacuum.

Every high school senior would be required to travel abroad by themselves, not as part of any academic program. They would need to figure everything out on their own and find a job in a foreign country.

When noticing a loud grinding sound while driving, turning the radio up would actually fix the problem.

Grade schools through middle schools would rotate assigned seating in the lunchroom. You want that PB&J and juice box? Sit next to a different stranger weekly and chat that kid up.

No one working at a nonprofit organization could ever haul in a million-dollar salary.

Cleaning one cat box would burn five thousand calories.

After two hours of screen time on your phone it would immediately shape-shift into a book in your hands. The only way to get service back would be to read the entire book.

Ice cream trucks should be able to choose their own music. Some suggestions: NIN, Hank Williams, NWA, and Andrea Bocelli.

Setting boundaries as an adult would only be perceived as an act of kindness and self-preservation.

Broken hearts can be fixed with a simple remedy found at a Minute Clinic near you. You'd get the additional privilege of two hours of extended playtime with a baby panda bear.

If given an introduction, Griffin Dunne and I would be friends.

Every internet troll who comments, especially on a *Star Tribune* article, should have to use their real name and a current photo.

Do away with all television advertisements that feature women romancing chocolate as a substitution for sex and replace them with Weird Al.

Every person who chooses not to go to the latest superhero blockbuster movie will be rewarded with lifetime immunity to urinary tract infections.

Judy Blume would be President. Amy Schumer Vice President.

Cadillac would bring back fins.

Some perfumier would capture the scent of apartment building dryer exhaust.

After every yearly pap smear, I would be handed a stunning antique lampshade as a parting gift.

Mick Jones and Joe Strummer would have made one more record together after *Combat Rock*.

Dead-end jobs would have an intuitive ejection seat that would hurtle you into space at 5Gs when you need to make a change.

Every DMV would have a light-up *Saturday Night Fever* dance floor as well as a fog machine. The only way you advance your number being called is by how much booty shaking you've put in.

Shoe/boot designers create and manufacture pairs where one shoe is a half-size bigger.

Everyone would still have a crush on their partner, however long you've been together.

I would never suffer another unripe cantaloupe. This would also be helpful in curbing my unnerving violent fantasy to throw bad fruit back through the grocery store window from whence it came.

Dog parks would be the only place animals become verbal, speaking to each other, and expressing their thoughts clearly, finally revealing that your pooch's speaking voice sounds like Renée Zellweger or Leon Redbone.

Everyone would own a motorcycle or convertible at some point in their lives.

I'd like to introduce the expression "Janky Tits" as an acceptable description when a situation is truly messed up.

Both Buddy Holly and Amy Winehouse would've lived and made music for another sixty-five years.

When selecting a Lyft ride pickup, you can choose a pony ride instead of a white Hyundai.

All utility bills and student loan statements come with five lottery tickets and a cold can of Diet Coke.

My black vintage horsehide jacket that was stolen from the Entry dressing room would reappear at my door. Tucked in its pocket: a love note from the Verve's Richard Ashcroft.

Senior citizen bingo is a televised Olympic sport.

If we all led life with curiosity instead of fear.

Everyone would know that "Cum On Feel the Noize" was written by Slade. Not Quiet Riot.

10

911 IS A JOKE

ONE MORNING BEFORE WORK I CHECKED MY CELL PHONE AND THERE were two messages from an unknown number.

The first message was sent on a Tuesday at 11:34 p.m. Never having heard Shit Bag's voice, my body started to shake. The overfamiliar tone that I had become so resentful of in his written letters was on full display. I could barely stomach listening to it in its entirety. I caught something about, "Hey sweetheart, it's Patrick, I'm getting into the shower; wish you were in it with me."

Second message: "I want to hear your voice before I go to bed."

My head was swimming. How did he get my number? I didn't even want to handle my phone for fear of accidentally calling him back. I handled it like a live grenade.

I raced into work early and headed straight to the lawyer's office. "He's got my personal phone number and he called twice last night. Please help me." They called the local police, who came into the station.

I sat there waiting for St. Paul's finest to show up while trying to make small talk with the lawyer who had thanked my stalker for being a member of public radio.

Huddled around a conference table my cell phone messages were played for the five people in the room. He began to describe in detail about me being on my knees sucking him off in the shower. I was mortified.

It was the first time I listened to them in their entirety. Searching those faces at the table I looked for one person to validate my fear. I wouldn't say anyone looked shocked. Maybe slightly uncomfortable.

THE POLICE OFFICER suggested I go down the street and file a restraining order immediately. You might be thinking, Why did it take so long to do this?

I didn't know his name for months; I still had no address, and when serving an order of protection, you need the creep's address.

Best I could do was apply for the restraining order prohibiting him from showing up at my work. This felt futile as the infiltration of his obsession had already moved on to me at home.

SITTING IN that government office an hour before I went on air felt surreal.

Nobody wanted to make direct eye contact. We were all here for the same reason, we needed an order of protection from someone threatening to hurt us.

Filling out those forms should've been my first clue to the uniqueness of filing a restraining order against a stranger. All the questions came with a presumption you knew the person on a more intimate level.

For the first time it felt like I was taking proactive measures. The feeling of being helpless with no allies was growing inside of me like a tumor.

IN ORDER TO FILE an order of protection you must write details in your petition form. This is verbatim from the actual form:

> the Respondent has physically or sexually assaulted you (only one incident is required); or
>
> the Respondent used your personal information, without your consent, to invite, encourage, or solicit a third party to engage in a sexual act (only one incident is required); or

the Respondent shared private sexual images of you without your permission (only one incident is required); or
the Respondent has made repeated acts, words, or gestures; and the actions have caused, or were intended to cause, substantial adverse effect upon your safety, security, or privacy.

Naturally, my next question is, how to serve the stalker when you don't have any known address? Here's where it gets mind-numbingly complicated.

In Minnesota, service is usually done by law enforcement ("peace officer"), but it could also be done by a corrections officer, such as a probation officer, court services officer, parole officer, or an employee of a jail or correctional facility. As an alternative, the law allows a peace officer to serve the respondent with a "short-form notification" that notifies the respondent of the basic elements of the order. This may be appropriate, for example, if the respondent comes into contact with the police and the police learn that there is an unserved temporary restraining order. The short-form notification will have the following instructions to the respondent: "The restraining order is now enforceable."

Oh, and YOU have to pay to file a restraining order! Walking out of there didn't make me feel any safer. At best, if he didn't already own a firearm, it's possible he might be flagged if they check the system for outstandings while he's legally procuring a handgun.

If the person cannot be physically located, a judge can authorize the clerk of the court to serve by certified mail or, rarely, by publication in a newspaper.

Janky man. I never understood that part. A restraining order might be published. Where exactly?

Better Homes and Predator?

I don't want to bog you down with the minutia of these laws I still can't comprehend. I guess the key word in all of this is *served*. I'm no expert but just the act of filing is no assurance that it can or ever will be served. So, every other person in that government office that day filling out the same wretched paperwork, who was scared out of their mind by another person's threats, was also not guaranteed safety. None of this is up front or clearly explained.

Thinking about it I want to take a hostage.

Sleep tight and sweet dreams.

Plenty of times I'd begin my radio show with a "Here's a funny thing I did before coming to work" story.

There was so little I could share with listeners. Calling the cops and having explosive diarrhea was my new morning routine.

I felt as if it was my first time opening a mic to speak. It all felt disingenuous, while still being at that point nobody's business but mine.

After the disturbing phone calls and the restraining order filing, I had to tell Potsy what was going on. This was something I was dreading. Void of empathy. I wasn't going to go into details, just the basics of I have a stalker that was getting more serious.

I had so little rapport or trust with him before all of this began. I couldn't stomach his competitiveness with me. This is my supposed boss. I'm going to confide my deepest fears to this dude.

I would rather drink hot dog water.

Trying to keep my voice from shaking, I explained the basics without a lot of detail but emphasized the sexual nature of his voice mail messages. I can tell you for a fact that one of his reactions was a head shake and the comforting word.

Weird.

I understand that if you haven't been in this position where your personal safety was at risk from a stranger you might not have the adequate words to offer support.

Weird will never be the response anyone is looking for.

The next Sunday afternoon was one of those perfect warm days when you could fly your windows open. I was putzing around when I saw a man walk with purpose up my front walk.

I have a four-season front porch and a dining room window that looks into the porch. I started to tremble. I had no idea what this stalker looked like but instinctually I knew it was him.

How do I describe this feeling of a stranger at my home?

I'm hiding and my gut is screaming at me that this is the man who is about to turn your world upside down. I ducked beside my window frame out of sight of the front door. This idiot rang the bell several times, while the dogs went ape-shit barking.

If you're standing outside at my door, you can see into my porch. I heard him talking to my dogs through the screen window. I went cold. This was the fucker who had mentioned my dogs and a possible unforeseen accident befalling them. He stood there for what seemed like ten years; I peeked to see a small part of the back of his head finally turning away from my door.

In that moment I wasn't thinking about getting a really good look at him for future ID lineups. I wanted to dissolve on the spot. I didn't want to look directly at him or commit any features to memory. He was a blob, a blurry threat.

This was a whole next level of anxiety. It was no longer contained to work. It was at my front door, looking into my windows.

In hindsight it also blew my mind that on this, my first experience with him at my house, he didn't leave any festering gift on the stoop. This was a pop-in visit.

His intention was for me to swing open the door and welcome him inside?

THIS SHOULD GIVE YOU some idea of how unclear I was thinking: I called my manager Potsy on his home phone. This part I will never forget: the entirety of my conversation with him while coming unglued, he was pumping air into a basketball.

Again, I'm not condemning anyone who doesn't know what this feels like—of course they don't unless it's happened to them. But here's where empathy can go a long way. Maybe even take notice that your employee is audibly upset to the point where you might stop what you're doing for five minutes to listen and maybe call for a wellness check.

Correct me if I'm wrong, but "Bummer" should not be the proper response to any of what I was saying.

So now we've got *Weird* and *Bummer.*

OVER THE NEXT FEW WEEKS, the creep's home visits amped up to several times a week.

Before all of this I didn't like anyone walking up to my front door, not boy scouts, canvassers, pizza delivery. That's my quirk. I had a NO SOLICITING sign on my front door that you could see from space. I made a custom welcome mat that read, THERE IS NO REASON FOR YOU TO BE HERE.

The number of times there was a police squad car in front of my house was becoming frequent. I started the blue card collection. If you're unfamiliar, anytime 911 is called with responding officers they leave you with a blue case card.

I always preemptively met the officers on the sidewalk with my copy of the restraining order in hand. Odd detail: they never really looked at my papers. Do I watch too many movies? Shouldn't they have at the very least run his name into their system to see if he was on probation or an axe murderer that had eluded capture?

I didn't really know any of my neighbors, as I'm surrounded by high-turnover rentals. I can't imagine what people's guesses were as to why Johnny 5-0 was making so many visits to this radio spinster's overgrown house that nobody ever saw leave. Maybe they thought I was sleeping with a cop.

I would drive in front of my house on my way home from work, to prepare myself for something sitting on my front stoop.

The one time Shit Bag had just left a bag of trauma on my front stoop the cops showed up relatively quickly, and as we were standing there, me consolidating my story for the millionth time with every new cop, the Shit Bag slowly cruised down the street right in front of us. I yelled, That's him! The officers there didn't blink.

I had an instinct to start running after the car. And then what?

I could not recognize the person I was becoming. Unhinged.

Letters and envelopes were now appearing in my backyard, hand-placed on my back step. My backyard had always been a sanctuary; despite being a pet cemetery, it was private and small. First thing I had done when I bought the house was contract a privacy fence company to build before I had moved in. Sends a nice message to neighbors; hi, I'm your new neighbor, I'm building a tall fence, you'll never have to see me.

Now it was getting closer and more aggressive. He was walking around my house, opening my gate, and leaving his "gifts" inches from my back door. A pile of black dirt on the stoop with a sympathy card resting on top.

The feelings of violation became overwhelming, and my imagination ramped up. Did he just place it there? Is he in the alley around a corner? Is he watching me? His letters indicated that he knew where I was always and what I was doing and with whom.

I had apparently become a huge whore during this period. Classic case of when you don't respond even one time to someone's advances, they build up in their head a whole story about how unworthy you are. Your lack of response is driving this person's imbalance off the charts.

I had confided in my older brother Paulie.

He's a one-of-a-kind thinker, somewhat unreliable and a loose cannon in the best way, and has a knack for knowing when to rally and come out of his rabbit hole for me.

I got him up to speed. It felt amazing to speak freely with someone I've known my entire life. We didn't often have these kinds of conversations, but I felt I was being heard. Spilling my guts out to my brother for the first time maybe ever, expressing my humiliation, diving deep into the dysfunctional family history. Showing him my most authentic self, questioning if I should check myself in somewhere because I was feeling suicidal.

He listened for an hour and thoughtfully offered up these words, "You know what you need?"

I sat rapt, waiting for the sage wisdom.

"You need a better TV, the one you have is shit."

Okay. Wait, what?

He asked if I had the creep's phone number, which I did.

As he took the number down and knowing what I know about my brother, his methods not always being sound, I knew he was going to call him. What was that going to sound like? If after telling him I'm feeling like offing myself, to which his best solution is upgrading my television, what on earth was he going to say to this mentally unstable barnacle?

Having older brothers, there is always a hint of that Sonny Corleone "You hit my sister?" protectiveness. To this day he won't tell me what he said, only that it was on his voicemail. "It's not what I said, but how I said it."

Immediately, I flashed-forward to this recording being played in court and somehow being used against me. Truthfully, having wingnut friends and family who offer up vigilante type of action was something I was okay with. Nothing else worked. Why not?

I CALLED MY BROTHER early one evening to hop on his bike to come over (he doesn't drive) after an arrangement of weeds and dead grass in a vase had been left on my doorstep while I was at home.

I can't describe the feeling of being there when he was creeping around my yard, sickened I had just missed him or that he was lurking around a corner.

I didn't know where to stand in my house or what to do while waiting. Avoiding windows and being self-conscious that my odd behavior was at some point going to affect my pets. Why is mom darting around the house crouching under windows with a baseball bat in her hand?

My brother did finally show up, and his predictably unpredictable solution was to take the glass vase of yard clippings and hurl it into the street. Figuring if the creeper was still around, he might be put off by his gift being rejected as a projectile missile shattering in the road.

That all seems so innocent in retrospect. We were thinking of him as a regular person who would be frightened off by someone pitching a glass vase into the street. Then you have to think, Wait, we're dealing with a guy who ripped up grass clippings and carried a vase around to leave it on a stranger's stoop that they believed they were having a sexual relationship with.

Can we out-crazy CRAZY? *Formidable* is not the right word. I was up against an unknown force of mental illness that acted fearlessly. All I could do was sink deeper into the dank hole that had burrowed inside of me.

ANOTHER NIGHT after a bold visit—a plastic Target bag filled with used children's toys outside my back door—I had enough skin crawling.

Coming to the front door was horrible enough. Taking the next nervy step in walking around the narrow side of my house and letting himself into my fenced backyard was too much too handle.

I found myself frantically searching the yard for poison. What am I even looking for? Chocolate bars? Cyanide dog treats? When someone threatens your dogs and they might be in danger of poisoning, you start acting like a lunatic. Picking up petrified poop with your bare hands to double-check it's not a Snickers bar.

MY BROTHER CARLOS offered to stay at my house, and I checked into a cheap hotel. Don't for a second think that I wasn't assuming he was probably following me in my flight to safety.

I barely had ninety minutes of fitful sleep in this crap hotel with Burger King orange nubby drapes. The next morning I had to go directly to work. When I got home the next afternoon the scrawled note said there had been no further signs of a visit and that my brother had taken one of my vintage leather coats as payment for standing watch.

I kept a notebook on the dining room table that held our ongoing messages to each other. I ate your frozen pizza. No sign of the creeper. Your cats are indoor cats, right?

When I returned home after these cheap hotel escapes my brothers would have all my blinds drawn and the TV would be on full blast. I had to snicker once as one of them had left the Golf Channel on at top decibel. Of all channels to sound intimidating to potential unwanted visitors. Polite clapping?

I also have a friend who has been known to head-butt a stranger while drunk who offered to sleep in my backyard. I seriously contemplated it. The mere suggestion of something so ridiculous felt like a tender offering, one that I would cherish.

11

YOU CAN'T PUT YOUR ARMS AROUND A MEMORY

TRAUMA COMES IN MANY FORMS AND TO DIFFERENT DEGREES. IF YOU don't know me, which you probably don't, here's a little backstory.

One recent holiday season, I found myself digging for vinyl at the Electric Fetus for potential gifts. I've always loved record-store culture. Some of my favorite humans work at record stores. But this was a *major* step for me.

I can count on one finger how many times I've been record-store shopping in the past decade, as my tragic relationship with vinyl haunts me to this day. Years ago, an unthinkable event occurred—a situation I was in no way prepared to handle.

You live in an apartment building, and you go downstairs to use the laundry room. Normal day, maybe even a good day. Trust and believe the last thing on Earth you want to see is *this* handwritten note on the bulletin board: "Whoever has storage space #11, the water pipe overhead burst, possibly over a week ago. Check for damage."

With that one message, I knew my life had changed.

My lifetime collection of vinyl was floating in sewage. I felt like I had taken a tire iron to the side of my head. I couldn't even bring myself to unlock the padlock and inspect the carnage right away.

I'm not Gandhi. I like my material things. I shed tears over a 1930s velvet fainting couch that my cat used as a toilet. In perhaps a very telling detail about myself, I have to get rid of whatever it is in my life that is ruined. There will be no trying to fix the problem, even if it means I will drag a hundred-pound sofa down three flights of stairs by myself to get the object out of my sight. Rigor mortis has set in, the body is starting to stink, it must be buried.

Standing in a pool of dirty water looking at my mildewed record collection was more painful than viewing an open casket. Reality came sharply into focus: I had lost a huge part of my identity, plain and simple.

The first records I bought with my own money as a kid, the inherited collection from older siblings and parents, gifts from friends, amazing thrift-store finds, expensive picture discs, imports, rare twelve-inches, crappy music purchased solely for album artwork . . . I was no longer the person who owned them and had moved them from apartment to apartment, city to city, for so many years. They were the butt of a joke among friends who dreaded helping me move each time. I may have moved around like a hobo, but I didn't travel light.

Like anyone who has lived through a fire, the thought of *What do I do now?* pounded in my brain. Starting over seemed out of the question—and far too depressing. I did not have the will to re-create my youth.

That's exactly what it felt like to me.

So many well-meaning friends have offered to help me acquire a "new" collection. That would never be the same. Should I also recreate my baptism, repeat high school, and re-virginate?

I remember where I got my records, the experiences of garage sales, walking with the brown paper bag under my arm.

It was all defining who I would become. The excitement of dropping the needle, the crackle, the burst of scratchy guitars.

Though this happened many years ago, I was still a grown-up and had to make some impossible decisions. I called several record-store clerks in town with my sad list of inventories, choking back tears to hear their assessment of the monetary worth. To their credit, they were all very gentle with me and very understanding, even going out of their way to not make a big deal out of some of the particularly devastating losses. They were my grief counselors.

Next, I had to call the undertaker (my insurance company), realizing it was a pointless endeavor to plead my case about the importance of owning a copy of *Cocksucker Blues*. I listened to this square from the insurance company detachedly doing his job, and I accepted his woefully modest offer of compensation.

On a bright note, I consoled myself with the fact that one amazing collector's item I proudly owned wasn't floating in my underwater renters' dungeon: I had loaned my copy of Prince's The Black Album (bought under the counter) to a friend one summer, back in the day when a friend would borrow a record to tape it for themselves.

After a few weeks, I inquired about it, and my stoner pal sheepishly admitted he left it in his car, which had been sitting in the impound lot for fourteen days in July.

The feeling of having to identify a decaying body at the morgue came over me. Did I want to visit the lot and have a sheet lifted from his rusted Honda Accord, just to see this melted masterpiece now in the shape of a gravy boat? The answer was *no*.

The double blow was that I was set to move once again and had just hauled my entire collection to the storage locker only a month before the tragedy. Akin to having been thrown from a horse, or having your heart broken, or maybe having your heart broken by a horse and then set on fire: the spook was in full force.

I gave my stereo to a friend. I locked the padlock to the vinyl crypt and never opened it again. I left my entire drowned former life exactly as it was the day I found it submerged. I moved.

I'm still unsure if I actually "moved on," as it still pains me to walk into record stores and see people flipping through crates, eagerly adding to their own identity as I did for so many years.

Not long after I started at The Current, I got an email from someone who had moved into my old apartment and had inherited my storage locker. The person was kindly—and I'm sure, confused as hell—asking me if I wanted to retrieve the contents. I couldn't even respond. I deleted the message and, with that, finally deleted a part of my history.

12

HEY HO! LET'S NOT!

I DON'T LIKE BEING TOLD WHAT TO DO.

This does not make me an ideal candidate for holding 99 percent of all jobs with a boss, nor does it increase the likelihood of me joining a cult.

Having Instagram "followers" even sounds a bit suss. Maybe we should substitute the word *freaks* for *followers*. I guess they both mean the same in the end. Better yet, maybe a completely innocuous term should be substituted like *stretch pants*—that way Megan Thee Stallion can brag that she has 2.7 million stretch pants.

How often in life is there a person telling you what to do whose ideas you have genuine respect for? A person with a vast imagination and staggering intellect who exceeds all of your own collective smarts. It's safe to say I've never had Maya Angelou for a supervisor.

For me it's always been the diametric opposite. The person giving some useless directions, not only do I not respect them, but I don't necessarily even like them. That's when my inner voice is ball-gagged and I have to politely listen as if I might actually be considering the buffoon's suggestions.

It's at this point when a cartoon balloon should appear above my head reading, "I don't remember asking you a goddamn thing."

Does this make me an insufferable clown that always knows best?

Far from it. A lifetime of sticking my neck out for possible beheading is my choice. I've always believed that my initial intuition is the direction I should follow. That way the failures (F.A.I.L. = First Attempt in Learning) and successes rest on my shoulders.

I ONCE HAD a restaurant manager whom I genuinely loved. His position of leadership and easygoing requests were always delivered with humor, so I never viewed him as an authority figure.

Come to think of it, he didn't hide his own disdain for THE MAN, so there wasn't any bootlicking behavior or suggestion that he respected the owner of the place. No "Let's work our tails off to make this fool richer than he already is."

When seating customers, he would ask their seating preference of smoking or nonsmoking and then sometimes under his breath offer the alternate choice of being hacked to death with a kitchen knife.

That is the way to my heart. Dark humor mutterings.

I was a wretched server, I should add. It's the only occupation that haunts my recurring dreams to this day. Trying to put my food orders into the computer with fingers like a canned ham. I have five hundred tables seated angrily waiting for water and menus. The Goo Goo Dolls are blasting from the boom box in the kitchen.

I asked this beloved manager to write me a letter of recommendation for another job I was pursuing, and he wrote two versions. One for me and one for the pending new employer. The second letter was filled with glowing lies and false descriptions of my commitment and top-shelf skills as a server.

The letter meant for my eyes only said, "Lucia is a delight to work with, that is *when* she actually works and hasn't traded away the majority of her shifts to other more competent employees. Her idea of side work is smoking near the dumpster with a full section. I've never seen her bus a table. I believe she would rather lick a dog's ass. I'd hang out with her if I wanted to score weed. Hire her and you will be sorry. P.S. Check her apartment for stolen cutlery."

I still fantasize about sending that letter attached to my current résumé.

I HAVE HAD a couple of good shrinks that after a certain amount of therapy, I've flat out asked them to tell me what to do about problems A, B, and Z. Paying someone two dollars a minute for their time, I figure they can occasionally pony up with some answers.

I am also not hesitant to ask the veterinarian what they would do if we were dealing with their own cat or dog. Screw liability: just tell me what to do as a kind fellow human. I will also abide by whatever my auto mechanic, Todd, tells me to do, simply because I don't know a serpentine belt from a seat belt.

Other than that, I don't usually ask for advice or direction from anyone.

I HAVE A VAGUE UNDERSTANDING of the adult person who might be more susceptible to joining a cult. Directionless, lacking imagination, a need to belong that supersedes rational thought.

My theory is most cult leaders are actually failed musicians or artists. At first there might initially be a whiff of bohemian appeal but dig a little deeper until you uncover the sociopath.

It's all fun and games while some gakked-out hippie is strumming a guitar telling you how special you are. Welcome to your new family! Next thing you know, you're in a flaming compound jumping out an eighth-story window in Nikes with a shaved head and permanent Kool Aid mustache waiting for the spaceship to retrieve you.

This next sentiment I realize may sound obnoxiously intolerant and controversial.

Is it religion bashing or just cult curious?

As much as I love the music of Beck, there has always been a part of me that can't help questioning his decision to follow the teachings of a half-baked science fiction writer with pink eye. As always, whatever gets you through the night. Clearly it works for him. He seems to be a true individual thinker creatively. Which doesn't translate as cultastic.

It's difficult to get my head around this unique artist who gave us *Odelay* and *Midnight Vultures* would've at some point considered signing a billion-year contract of loyalty to a self-proclaimed deity named Ron.

As usual you can find most of my personal feelings and theories at the corner of NO and SHIT.

13

ARE YOU SURE YOU'RE HIS TYPE?

LET'S CONTINUE WITH THE GASLIGHTING, SHALL WE?

My experience with the Minneapolis Police ramped up to requests for help at home, sometimes three times a week.

This would be my education on how ill-equipped law enforcement is when dealing with a case of nondomestic stalking. There was a blatant disregard for the seriousness of the stalker's consistent appearances at my home and in my yard, the junk he left on my doorstep.

More than one responding officer took it upon himself to comment, "Those are nice flowers, he must be a big fan."

Everything I tried to explain was met with the most dismissive "We got real crimes to solve, lady" attitude. More thinking out loud than direct conversation, I obsessed on the confusion of how he knew where I lived. One sensitive officer dismissed my worry by saying, "I wouldn't get bogged down by that: he probably followed you home from work."

I stared at the idling squad car and zeroed in on To Protect and Serve.

I THINK IT BEARS REPEATING that every single time he showed up at my house I called 911, and each time I had to retell the story, which from the jump seemed to confuse the responding officers. No, I don't know him. This has been going on for over a year. I had a copy of the restraining order by the door. I should've had the condensed version down by then. But I was always so rattled I couldn't whittle it down to three sentences.

One time he had left a note with a religious candle. The policeman asked me how I knew it was from the same guy. I said I'm beyond familiar with his handwriting, and he interrupted with, "Oh, are you a handwriting expert?" Yes, in fact I am. Are you an expert douchebag?

Sleep became dodgy for me, and one night I woke to the sound of glass breaking. I have Pugs, they snore and breathe like James Gandolfini, so I wear earplugs. This I heard clear as a bell.

I thought, this is it. He's in my home. I didn't want to turn a light on in the house. Funny thing was, I had just recently purchased an illegal monster-watt bulb for my front door motion light. The dude at the hardware store was hesitant to sell it to me. I wasn't feeling the contraband vibe as he went into a closet to produce the biggest honking light bulbs I'd ever seen.

Explaining why they weren't to be sold, he said it was partly environmental, and being banned for casting too much light for a residential property. He wasn't kidding: this thing could light Yankee Stadium. Every innocent dog walker or squirrel got a blast of light like Poltergeist.

As a housewarming present when I first moved in, my older brother had gifted me with a baseball bat. I grabbed my Louisville slugger, which I now slept with, and crept down the stairs in boxer shorts and a Motorhead T-shirt.

I saw that my front storm door was swung open, and the glass window was shattered all over the front steps. I called 911 and tried the abbreviated version of my spiel: I have a stalker who has broken the restraining order countless times, I was awakened to the sound of breaking glass. They dispatched the coppers, and I waited on the front porch; to avoid knocks on doors and barking dogs I usually went out to meet them.

Terrified and trying to look like I wasn't broken inside, I started into my story. The officer interrupted me to scold me—more importantly—about my illegal light bulb. Really? You're going to lecture me about that while standing in a pile of glass at 3 a.m.? He then seemed to shift his gaze to me standing there. Taking in my appearance, he asked, "Are you sure you're his type?" What the actual!?

He then asked . . . wait for it . . . if I had a husband.

Because that would solve everything, and married people don't get stalked? I was speechless. Is this going to be the moment I tell the MPD to eat a bag of dicks?

Paranoid or not, it wasn't the first time there was some snide inference made based on my appearance: I wasn't worthy to be stalked. I might have looked a little too punky for them to believe I could be the subject of this unwanted attention. Plus, I was in my early forties, for crying out loud. Expired goods.

After they left, I sat on my front porch in the dark holding that baseball bat tight.

I'm the least violent person you can imagine. I slammed a door once while angry and felt horrible for weeks after. My racing thoughts were creating the scenario in which he would return to my front stoop, and I would fling the door open and start bashing his head in.

This stopped me in my tracks. I have never had such visceral thoughts of violence in my life and now I was choreographing bludgeoning his skull in detail.

Again, whose life am I living? I was pushed to a place so unfamiliar that it frightened me.

A stranger is doing this to me. He has stripped away so much of who I had been. Nobody can help me. Nobody understands what this feels like.

Well-meaning friends tell you how strong you are as a means of comfort, and you'll get through this. I felt quite differently. I am not strong.

What doesn't kill me just makes me weirder and harder to relate to.

A beautiful friend sent me this:

> Your trauma made you stronger.
>
> No, my trauma made me traumatized, it made me weak, gave me sleepless nights, and memory loss. It gave me feelings I've never wanted.
>
> I made myself stronger, by dragging myself out of a dark place, and dealing with consequences that weren't my fault.

I don't know who to attribute these wise words to, but I feel every one of them.

THROUGHOUT THE LAST YEAR I had heard about a local TV reporter who had a stalker. She's beautiful and blonde. It was later revealed he had taken his own life when authorities had served him his restraining order. In my twisted framework I thought how lucky she was, even to the point of feeling envious. Why couldn't my mentally unstable stalker do the same? Being a person of compassion, the nature of these real feelings of wishing someone would solve my problem by offing himself gives you an idea of how much I was changing. God, I resented that.

Members of my own family did not take this seriously. It wasn't because they didn't want to cause further stress by sympathizing with the scariness of the situation. It just felt like a dismissal I was already well familiar with: you're the baby of the family and you don't know what you're talking about.

More than once it was suggested with a laugh and a sigh, "Only you, Looch."

Oh, how I wished people wouldn't say that. In that state of mind and trying to make any kind of sense of this nonsense I did start thinking, Did I draw this upon myself somehow? Was I too good at relating and connecting with strangers that for every hundred real fans there is also a mentally unwell listener who believes that you are only speaking to them?

I'd been fairly confident that what made me stand out in this career was my ability to connect with strangers through storytelling or honestly owning up to being a genuine buffoon. Trying to wrap my head around the idea that these abilities that came second nature to me were also a primary reason that something like this would naturally *only* happen to me.

Overwhelmed, there were plenty of times I wanted off this planet.

MY PRIMARY DOCTOR was an elegant mature woman who loved new music and attended concerts that the station promoted. I had been seeing her throughout all of this and she knew where all the bodies were buried. Once while doing a band intro, I spotted her in the crowd and shouted her out from the stage, suddenly feeling like Brian Wilson minus the terry cloth bathrobe.

Yo! Give it up for Dr. Walker! What the hell am I doing?

Let me say this about sweet Dr. Walker, who wasn't my shrink but was well versed in my status and treating my PTSD with various methods. After another news story was published about him being arrested again, this woman called me at home to see if I was all right.

Let that sink in.

A doctor in the year 2014 called me at home, checking up on me out of concern, and gave me her private number.

Solid Gold.

14
SISTER MORPHINE

My oldest sister, Anne (Sister Morphine), was almost seventeen years older than I. I wouldn't say we had an easy relationship. We were very different people with different experiences.

That's cool. I didn't grow up in a traditional family. We didn't grow up together so much as around each other. By the time I was born she was out of the house. We experienced family differently. I get it.

Before this stalker, we were superficially chummier and could find laughs in certain things. She loved animals and the Ramones. Down deep I hoped like hell that on someone's deathbed it wouldn't be revealed she was my biological mother.

At some point something changed in me, in her, in the world around us. I was more comfortable remembering her as my hippie oldest sister who had a talent for drawing and landscape design. She began parroting some of my mom's jabs. She always had strong opinions about other people. Judgy Wudgy Was a Bear.

She was witheringly self-deprecating, which eventually lost its intended humor and seemed a thin veil for her actual pain. I could see that. A blind man could see that. She became an angry person who had a razor-sharp tongue, though to an outsider I'm sure it was viewed as caustic humor. But lord help you if it was ever directed at you. With me she took direct aim.

While I was at work one day, she came over to work on my backyard. I didn't ask her to but thanked her profusely for watering the things I had neglected. She apparently tripped in my yard and hurt her shoulder. The next thing I knew she sent me the most scathing letter, threatening to sue me for permanent physical damages due to her fall.

She also sucker-punched me with a cavalcade of nonsense about how I was "mishandling" being stalked. I apparently hadn't read her manual on the correct response to feeling terror. She questioned why my employer would hold my job for me while I was on leave.

As much as I've thought about it over the years, I have no idea what happened or changed in her. At the lowest point in my life, she went after me with both barrels. I can never make sense of it. The relationship felt hopeless to navigate.

I eventually wrote her a letter explaining that her words were vicious, and I was beyond confused where it was coming from. I didn't bring up her threat to sue me. Her response was a text message that said, jokingly (maybe?): "I guess in my older age I've become more of a bitch."

We didn't see each other often after that but I was always friendly. Guarded but cordial.

Setting boundaries as an adult is never without consequence. Especially with family. You're thinking of self-preservation. They think, "You cold bitch."

That you learn to live with. It hurts. Somehow, you're hurting the person causing you harm. I truly believe rage disfigures the soul; I've been on the receiving end. It's taken a lot of compassion, questioning, and inward thinking to finally realize someone else's anger has literally nothing to do with you.

I've been with people who are dying to live and those who are living to die. I have the utmost respect for either battle, as it requires an unbelievable amount of strength.

My sister landed in the hospital with a staph infection, which became sepsis, and things rapidly grew worse.

Being high-Covid time limited the number of visitors she could have. We all took turns hanging out with her. I took time off of work and caught a few coherent days. One in particular, I began to plan a trip to NYC with her when she got out. I had to chuckle as she rifled off a wish list of things to be done if she ever got out—one being to get her eyebrows threaded and the second was to divorce her husband who was in the room. Let's go!

It was woefully obvious she wasn't getting out.

One of the most unsettling things that people don't often mention is the first time you enter someone's hospital room when you have literally never seen this person lying down in a bed. The shock is so simple. The intimacy is almost embarrassing. Their vulnerability is the most beautiful you've seen in years.

That purity is the part I am there for.

I will set homemade pasta next to your bed that you will never eat. I will sit in your room reading.

I will play Neil Young songs quietly from my phone. Occasionally, I will stare at your face searching for familiarity. I will touch your hand and whisper, "It's going to be okay," hoping like hell you are in a euphoric morphine haze. Thinking of John Lennon, saying everything will be okay in the end. If it's not okay, it's not the end.

I said goodbye to you in a shrink's office six years ago. Last October I said it at your bedside.

The complicated relationship I have with my mom could be its own book.

She has an aversion to anything that might require nurturing. Children, animals, relationships, hobbies, pets, plants, babies. She loves two things. Baseball and Men.

She was always especially critical of me, and I'm not the biggest fuckup in the family. Sometimes the jabs had humor, like when she referred to the color of lipstick I wore as the "inside of a goat's stomach."

Growing up with two parents who were deeply unhappy people

separate from one another and even more so together, I had a much closer relationship to my eccentric and drug-addicted dad, Hal.

When you're told as a child by your mother that she can't stand your father and you're just like him, it does a number on your head.

I get it. You don't like me.

Her childhood is heartbreaking, and don't think for a second that I wasn't deeply sympathetic toward her most of my adult life. Sexual abuse dismissed by her own mother made her deeply untrusting of women.

I tried getting her into therapy. We even went to see my shrink together once and she put on this front of protection. Denying everything. I'm surprised she didn't take any stock in his opinion. I mean he was a man, after all.

Fear seemed to motivate all her choices in life.

I knew where it stemmed from and agonized about it plenty. Finally coming to the realization that she was only capable of certain things, and they were limited as hell, I gave up on trying to help. Her coldness toward me I've accepted as her own limitation. I know I've done nothing to warrant it.

I get that some people are not comfortable with any physical affection. Trying to embrace her was like hugging a garden rake. I will choose to keep a healthy distance from her negativity. Though when in crisis, naturally it would be nice to have a mother who cared.

FOOLISHLY, I PUT ASIDE a lifetime of boundaries to confide in her about the daily fear I was living with. Even I couldn't have been prepared for her callous dismissal of my current situation.

"He's just a *fan,* lighten up."

When I tell you I let things slide for the most part, you must believe me. This felt like a fracture, the final attempt to desire comfort from this woman.

I HAVE AN UPSETTING MEMORY of her slapping me in the mouth as a kid while I was talking or being "mouthy," as she described it. The humiliation of being struck while talking and the indelible smell of basil and onions on her hand felt much like the silencing I was required to do throughout this ordeal.

Years of shoved-down feelings came out of me and even while telling her how much it hurt to hear her lack of understanding, I knew it was the last time I would ever be dumb enough to expect anything that resembled compassion from her again. I was done.

15

ABOUT THAT TIME MR. CHESWICK ATE A COUCH

While dealing with a stalker, life doesn't hit pause: you have to find the will to continue taking care of other things that present a challenge. Jerry Seinfeld once said something to the effect that dogs find all the best stuff at ground level—the problem is they don't have pockets to store their finds for a later date. Lacking impulse control, it's best in their minds to just eat whatever they see laying there at their unique vantage point. Despite this smorgasbord philosophy, never once has one of my cats or dogs even offered to chip in on the squillion-dollar emergency vet bills for these misadventures.

Some staggering statistic involving the root-cause mystery of an unwell dog is usually predicated on this question: "Did they eat something unusual?"

Uh, well, they're dogs, so I'm going with yes. Fer crying out loud, random trash consumption is listed under Special Skills on all dogs' résumés. Retrieving things out of my dogs' mouths has become a full-time job. (Later, we can cover the topic of pulling things out of a cat's ass, such as tinsel on Christmas morning. I blame all children's books illustrated with a cat gently playing with a ball of yarn.)

As animal parents, we quickly learn the long list of potential death traps that decorate our dwellings. I came out of the womb with the knowledge that chocolate is poisonous to a dog.

Rubber bands, tampons (not usually on the living room floor, mind you), string, ribbon, cellophane. Think of an everyday, inanimate, and otherwise benign object you're too lazy to pick up in the moment, then imagine the offending object getting twisted around your baby's intestines like a tourniquet.

I thought I was well aware of the standard primary risks—until I adopted Mr. Cheswick, that is. At nine months of age, he ate a bolt of upholstery fabric. Cheswick had been sliding under furniture and goofing around as a pup on the regular. Of course, what we didn't realize at the time is that the thin fabric lining that all sofas and chairs have hidden underneath their bottom sides is, apparently, dee-lish. I was too busy being scarred by his insatiable appetite for scarfing the bindings of my favorite books to investigate his fascination with dicking around under the couch.

Sitting and waiting at the emergency vet is not delightful. People try and keep focus to their own fur child, occasionally looking up as a new hysterical human comes in with their particular fur emergency. This doesn't feel like the time or place to make chitchat—this is not National Night Out. We're all here in the waiting room fighting tears, scared out of our wits, and most of us are already panicked about the impending bill.

"What's wrong with your dog?" is an innocent enough question to ask; however, my first impulse is not to answer civilly but, rather, to stab the unsuspecting asker. Now add a line jumper to this nerve-wracking equation. We all are familiar with the rules of after-hours animal care: first come, first served. Life-threatening cases jump the line. We're merciful when it comes to those pets and their owners. If it bleeds, it leads.

However, this one particular buttinski kept repeatedly checking into the front desk, loudly asking how much longer for her dog to be seen. She even offered to answer the front desk phone, hoping that her willingness to do someone else's job would somehow make her a special case. I felt sorry for her dog. She was a lemon.

I had already unfairly sussed out her pooch as a non–life-threatening patient. He was occasionally scratching his ear. She had already been scolded for letting Itchy off leash to wander the waiting room. Plus, I was here way before her, cradling a shaking Mr. Cheswick who hadn't eaten in a day, was throwing up black bile, and nearly tipped over just trying to stand.

The thankless position of the front-desk staffer is particularly fascinating to me, as their job seems unthinkable and a great reason to do drugs. Checking in freaked-out people, answering the constantly ringing phones, running back to the exam rooms. There should be a little something extra in their paycheck for that kind of stamina.

Just like a human hospital, finally your name is called, and you get to wait in the smaller room for a lifetime. At least behind a closed door, you can let it rip. Cry, console Mr. Cheswick, and bitch about the head case who thought she was waiting on line at Studio 54. Sure enough, first question out of the vet tech's mouth: "Did he eat something out of the ordinary?"

Never in my wildest imagination could I guess exactly what he'd eaten, but given his proclivity for literature, anything was possible, so I answered I didn't know for sure. Just feeling his little belly she instinctually knew there was something lodged in there that shouldn't be. All I could think of was *Curious George Goes to the Hospital*—the caper in which the naughty little monkey ate a puzzle piece. I consoled myself that story had a happy ending. Where is my big yellow hat?

Uncertainty and inconclusive tests push me to the brink of asking the unthinkable. If he was your dog, what would you do? Liability aside, please tell me what to do! I can't think of many instances in which my mental health is dependent on someone telling me what to do. The vet's humanity showed through when she said, "I would get him into surgery immediately to find out what is in there." Unlike Curious G, the X-ray didn't show a perfectly intact puzzle piece.

Best they could determine pre-surgery: a wad of black substance. Great. That doesn't sound at all scary.

All day I was dry-heave nervous waiting for the post-op phone call. Finally, word came he was out of surgery and ready to come home. The surgeon was never able to identify the black mass, but if they'd offered, I would've taken it home with me and done my own lab pathology.

Turns out, I didn't need to. Arriving home with a sleepy Mr. Cheswick, I instinctively got down on the floor and hoisted myself underneath the furniture. There were only fragments of that black fabric still clinging to the bottom of my eighty-six-inch-long sofa. Mystery solved.

Let this be your cautionary tale. Do not let your dog off their leash at Joann Fabrics, no matter their potential to become the next Alexander McQueen!

16

BREAKING UP WITH MINNEAPOLIS

HAVE YOU EVER BEEN STUCK? I MEAN CIRCUMSTANTIALLY PARALYZED. All throughout 2014 and 2015, on a daily basis, I had to remind myself to breathe.

My life had come to an unnerving place of exhaustion, which left me in desperate need of change. My lack of clarity and stagnating anxiety had me, in the words of David Byrne, "trying to find myself a city to live in." If I couldn't change my problems, I would at the very least relocate them.

It's a heavy crossroads when you start to take stock of your life and career and ask yourself, "What is really keeping me here? Is everything I thought to be right now terribly wrong?" Colored with overwhelming feelings that both my home and workplace felt like a crime scene, I simply did not know where I belonged anymore.

So I reached out to various friends in cities I tried to imagine myself thrift-store shopping in: Seattle, Boston, Memphis, and Austin. Which of these cities had the optimum Pug weather? If I could get a handle on that, then I could worry myself into inertia about finding a job. Radio is pretty much all I've ever done, but again: where on earth would I fit?

My friend Bob in Memphis asked me why I was "breaking up

with Minneapolis," which is an interesting way to put what I was contemplating. I thought about it and realized I just needed to feel safe, and if that meant hauling my ass to a new town and starting from scratch, that might be a risk I was willing to take. The irony was not lost on me that there is nothing safe about doing something so drastic.

My judgment was so wonky that at one point I contacted my realtor who sold me my current house to look for another place as if I could outrun this problem with local relocation.

I half-heartedly looked at a few places with him. My deal-breakers in finding a new home weren't natural woodwork, character, charm, fireplace. It veered more into security features.

Two-car garage, yeah yeah. Is there a moat?

I stood in each of those homes knowing deep down I didn't want to live there. While standing in a stranger's dining room I glanced out the side window and like a bad acid flashback swore I saw Shit Bag's head walk by. That gave me a pause and a sobering realization I was not going to solve any problems of harassment by physically moving into another house.

To give you an idea of my mental framework, my memoir's working title is NOTHING WORKS. That way, if it ever gets published, I know they can't file it in the self-help section. As in all stories about trying to outrun your problems, at some point common sense takes hold, and that voice that had been hammering at me to grab the critters and skip town subsided into a slightly less wingnut tone.

I ended up staying here. To this day, what it is that I love most about Minneapolis, my answer is, "New York."

DURING THIS TIME as I considered relocation, nearly every conversation starter rubbed me the wrong way.

"Would you be available . . . ?"

I promise you: this question rarely is followed by anything I would ever want to do. I've never heard it fleshed out with, "Would you be available to stuff hundred-dollar bills into your pockets while getting a scalp massage from Joe Perry and simultaneously raid Alison Mosshart's closet?" Instead, it's more along the lines of judge a battle of the bands, come in early, stay late, let someone who is really interested in getting into radio shadow you for a day.

Anything involving a parade, a name tag, children's activities, or a "brain pick." And if the word *camping* is suggested, I dry heave and flee.

Same goes for, "Would you be willing . . . ?"

Think about that one. Willing? The intention in that deadly question already suggests suffering: "Would you be willing to eat Thanksgiving dinner in the 7th St Entry bathroom with a sales rep from Comcast while watching films about vivisection?"

Here's another social dirty bomb: "I recently met someone who said they know/knew you."

Again, without fail, it's never a person you do actually know or want to know.

And *knew*? Run like hell. There is a good reason they are someone you knew, past tense. DEFCON 1 is "I met someone you once dated." I'm gone before the word *dated* has even left their pie hole.

The socially unacceptable coping mechanism I've adapted with these conversation starters is to literally disappear. I mean it: ask anyone who knows me well. I receive more text messages from friends who say, "Are you still here?" I usually receive these messages while I'm washing my makeup off in my bathroom at home in boxer shorts.

17

CREEPER'S PARADISE

After so much prodding, I finally got the company's help to install security cameras in front and back of my house, after being told ad nauseum by responding officers, "We can't do anything if we don't catch him in the act." He had broken the restraining order so many times since I filed.

My assessment was that it was never served to him in person, as we had no address for him, or he was fearless with nothing to lose. No potential consequence seemed to slow down his pursuit. It had been made abundantly clear that catching him in the act was the only way to move things forward, seeing as responding officers always seemed to just miss his last visit by minutes.

A camera was my only option. Hard evidence. Proof I wasn't losing my mind.

For a company so concerned with optics I would've thought if it was made public that their well-liked afternoon drive host was being hunted by a delusional listener, they might've been more interested in becoming involved earlier. It had always felt like a workman's comp injury. This trauma was a direct result of my job. Maybe even worse: I couldn't shake the feeling that because I was relatable on air, I had somehow brought this on myself. So the very reason I held community cred for more than twenty-five years was also the unwanted invitation a mentally unstable listener applied to his delusional ideas that he knew me. That he loved me, and I loved him.

I was bolstered by the involvement of my place of employment finally taking this seriously and ensuring the next step of protection by installing the cameras.

A couple of engineers from work came over to assist. All I could think of naturally was that he was watching the comings and goings of several people working on ladders installing a camera. When someone tells you they know your every move, rational or not, you believe them.

Finally, I was put in touch with a police sergeant. A woman. An angel.

She called me when I was on air, we discussed my situation in a very detailed way, she was soft-spoken and so understanding. The fact that every thirteen minutes I'd have to put the phone down mid-sentence to tell a witty story about Car Seat Headrest just piled on what had already been a surreal way to live. Maintain a job of entertainment and whimsy while operating on little sleep or food in abject fear.

I told her about my collection of blue cards. I had accumulated so many from 911 calls and still with no direct help in terms of serving him, seeking out his address, or making an arrest.

Finally, someone seemed as disappointed as I was by the inaction and length of time this was dragging out.

She made a home visit and treated me with respect and empathy. She was the first person who offered anything that remotely looked like help. For one, she advised me to stop reading the letters that were steadily being mailed and/or placed carefully in my backyard.

Treat everything as evidence. Don't open an envelope. Use plastic gloves and Ziploc bags.

I felt like an idiot that continuing to read his delusional letters was doing more harm to me than I realized. It is the most ominous feeling to be told you are being watched and followed. Constant warnings that you are in great danger.

The letters he wrote were grim and frightening. I wanted to stop beating myself up that I had let this stranger into my head. There was no avoiding it. His descriptions of knowing where I was at any given time during the day I believed. I kept reading these disgusting letters because when someone tells you that they are watching you and know your every move, you want to know if he's planning on coming over on Saturday afternoon.

Out of the need to know what his sick plans were for me, I did continue to read these letters. Keeping tabs on the person who has me in his crosshairs.

SHE ALSO BROUGHT along with her a home security specialist named Chanel. She was the kind of brassy broad I've always admired.

Chanel asked if she could see the outside of my house and yard while the sergeant and I were seated at my dining room table. I looked at her gentle features and then glanced down at the piece in her holster—such an odd juxtaposition.

She was thorough. I saw her head pass my side window trying to beat her way through the overgrown bushes peppered with the occasional, "Now ain't that some shit."

Her assessment of my pathetic attempt to create an unbreachable fortress was hilarious.

"Shit. This is a creeper's paradise. You gotta cut back those bushes and trees. Don't you want it to look like someone lives here?"

As far as the locks I had put on my back gates, they didn't pass muster with Chanel. "Girl, I got bigger locks on my luggage: what are you thinking?"

Feeling like Scarface's Tony Montana minus the mountain of blow, having two live video monitors in front of you gives you a weird sense of protection, but it also fuels the obsessive nature of noticing every moving object on camera. It was nice to be able to run interference on approaching Jehovah Witness solicitors and UPS deliveries.

THE MOST RECENT LETTER in my mailbox had a return address. Holy Hell! Had he slipped up? Was it intentional?

Upon opening it I was sickened at the now-familiar handwriting outlining that I was in deep trouble. It was coming for me because I was a whore. He would be the only one to SAVE me.

I did my routine of handling it with plastic gloves and placing it into a plastic bag. This time I called the sergeant directly.

Finally, I had an address, the one thing I had been waiting for.

A day or two later the police sergeant called to tell me she and the security officer were coming over for a photo lineup to ID Shit Bag.

Keep in mind, it had been months since I was hiding around my window, glimpsing only the back of his head leaving my front stairs. I had maybe half a second to see his face. I could not get this wrong. This was the first step in serving him in person and or making an arrest.

There is a real procedural feel to doing a photo identification lineup. It's harrowing enough with just photographs: I can't imagine having to do it in person behind the two-way glass.

The three of us sat at my dining room table.

She held the manila envelope and I was instructed to look at each photo one at a time, and when I was done studying to turn the photo over before examining the next one.

First thing that throws you is they are not all mug shots. Some photos could be from a state ID or driver's license, and who knows how recent they were taken? Never having gotten a good look at his face straight on, I felt even more pressure to get this right.

Once you've looked at the ten photos one at a time, you are allowed to look at them all again putting aside possible suspects and eliminating others by placing them face down. Naturally, they assemble photos of similar-looking people with one wildcard thrown in for good measure. I almost chuckled when I saw the obvious plant.

Out of all the photos there were two that stood out.

My heart was thrashing as I eliminated the eight photos and looked at the two remaining men's upturned photos my instincts were pulling me to.

In the one I was drawn to initially, the hair color didn't match up with what I remember seeing so many months ago. But given that I change the color of my hair monthly, I relied on my gut feeling and pointed to the photo of the man with the reddish-brownish hair.

The smile that crossed the angelic sergeant's face told me I had picked the right creep.

It's difficult to describe the feeling of relying on pure instinct in such a crucial moment. The relief, and the hope, that you might be even a tiny step closer to ending this nightmare.

I had identified his photo, they had his name and address, the next step was to warrant an arrest and serve him. Had I not had the sergeant's involvement helping me, I highly doubt things would've moved as quickly as they did.

Eliminating so much of the mystery and unknown details about this person was the first time I allowed myself to breathe. Before that, I wasn't so much breathing as I was vibrating.

The sergeant told me they would let me know when they served him and/or arrested him.

After the official photo ID, finally my place of employment implemented a security guard posted outside of my house twenty-four hours a day. Unmarked car with a dude looking at his phone for eight-hour shifts. I hope they were paid well.

I was grateful. Then some bizarre concern to make sure they were well supplied with snacks, beverages, and reading materials overtook me.

I was so thankful that someone was finally protecting me and taking this seriously, I overcompensated by many trips out to the security car with granola bars and ginger ale. Then naturally I freaked out, thinking, *Are they going to ask to use my bathroom?* That would add an extra layer of weirdness to a situation that was already crazy.

I just hoped they had a Snapple bottle to piss in.

My mail carrier Todd, who is the most thoughtful human being ever to hold this job, by now had some idea of what was going on at my house. How many court documents, subpoenas, and court date notifications were streaming to my house delivered by him.

One of the security guards told me that he had protectively gone to their car window to inquire why they were sitting in front of my house like the secret service. For your mail carrier to be aware enough to notice a car parked in front of your house and make an inquiry is beyond heartwarming to me.

THE NEXT COUPLE OF DAYS were mentally exhausting. Of course, I was working, acting like my life wasn't in the toilet.

The call came in while on air when I had a window of ten minutes. I called her back. The sergeant didn't give too many details other than he was arrested and that they had seized his computer; forensic evidence takes some time to fully process; however, the contents of various things in his apartment linked him obviously to being my stalker. Can you imagine not knowing what those items were? My imagination was running the gauntlet as to what he had that was so blatantly incriminating. She made a point of emphasizing that there was no question that what was found in his apartment was linked to me and that I shouldn't make any further inquiries. Maybe it was a good thing that I got no details.

ONCE A PERP is processed through the county jail, their information becomes public domain, including his full name and age.

You can check the web on the jail's roster to see bail and the charges. His were two felony counts of stalking and one terroristic threat. Bail was a measly ten grand. The defendant only needs to come up with 10 percent. That's not enough to make anyone feel safe. A thousand bucks and this freak is free.

Knowing that he was locked up for the first time in two years I felt safe. Like a giant exhale of poison.

Of course, I checked obsessively to see that nobody had posted his bond.

KNOWING VIRTUALLY NOTHING about him, I wondered, Did he have family, a spouse, children? Did he know anyone that thought sparing him from jail was worth a lousy Kenny G?

Six days of the best sleep I'd had in recent memory, POOF! Gone.

Apparently, he did have somebody willing to post bond. And just like that he was out.

He was free and on probation until a hearing could be scheduled. This was November 2014.

Whoever posted his bail must've thought they were helping him. I couldn't imagine anyone knowingly enabling a person with this sick behavior.

ANY RATIONAL HUMAN BEING would assume that since he's been pinched, processed, made bail, surely he's not brazen enough to continue his delusional pursuit.

That is where we all make the mistake of thinking for him.

What person in their right mind . . . is a predictable sentence starter: the problem is blatantly there.

Right mind? No. You're forced to almost think like someone who has no fear of law; their mental illness has convinced them that we have a relationship and now I've involved the police. I poked the hornet's nest.

The warnings of my impending danger from him came before he had spent a few nights in the pokey. Given this illogical thought process, had I just made things worse for myself?

THE NIGHT BEFORE THANKSGIVING is affectionately known as Drunksgiving. Bars do more sales on this particular night than New Year's Eve. People getting their drink on before passing the yams to their dick relatives.

I was in bed with my trusty baseball bat when I heard a thunderous noise downstairs: someone was trying to kick my front door in. This was just a week after the creep's release, so every dreaded feeling came rushing to the fore.

This time I had a security camera. I called 911. I could see fresh footprints in the recently fallen snow on my front steps. For the first time ever, the police came into my house. We were going to check the camera footage together. As my luck would have it, the rewind feature wouldn't work, so I only had the live picture on display. Another blue card was issued, and they left. I called an engineer at work on Thanksgiving morning, begging him to check my footage after his family feast. The best he could get was a grainy screen-grab photo. The person in question trying to kick my door in was wearing a huge Michelin man winter coat with a hood. I couldn't make out a face or gender. It wasn't until the following Monday that an engineer from work could look at live footage. Still perplexed as to their identity, one thing was certain: this person was loaded, as they nearly took a header off my steps when they weaved away.

It was written off as a rando drunk.

FOR WHATEVER REASON the one helpful thing my employer did do was set up a security camera at my house. What they didn't provide me with was a password that would allow me to access footage. Also, for the record, they stopped paying for it after a few months.

HE WAS OUT OF JAIL, free to move about the cabin, and the hearing date wasn't set until the following April.

I knew that I had hit the wall of what I was capable of doing at work. I had been silent so long it felt like I had been gargling Drano. My insides were shredded. I had to ask for a leave of absence to begin getting my head around what lay ahead.

At a staff meeting, which was normally mind-numbingly dull and without meaningful content, I sat in my chair thinking of how I would reveal to my coworkers what had been going on in my private life and how I didn't feel I could do the job that had always come so naturally to me. Potsy teed it up for me saying, "Looch has something she needs to share with you."

I looked down at my hands and tried not to cry. "I have a stalker" is how I started. "He's been bothering me for over a year, he's been to my house, and I'm terrified. He was finally arrested last fall. He made bail and is out on the streets again. A scheduled hearing is set for April. I need some time to prepare myself without the expectation of being on air everyday acting like nothing is wrong. I can't do it anymore."

Maybe three of my work friends already knew the situation. The rest of my coworkers looked shocked, but nobody said anything. What was there to say?

Truth be told, they were probably thinking, *I'm glad it's not me,* and that's not a knock on them.

18

ALONE WITH EVERYBODY

I KNOW I CAN'T BE THE ONLY ONE WHO FEELS LIKE THE HOLIDAYS ARE a big production of trying to jam my painfully round self into the square-shaped expectations of what celebrating Christmas should be.

It's never felt genuine. I'm not Grinch-y; it's just never mattered much to me, and pretending to be having a good time is soul sucking. Festive becomes festering.

I've spent a tedious amount of time doing things I did not want to do. That is an understatement, to say the least.

The past few Christmas Eves my family's tradition was gathering in the afternoon. With every invite I explained Christmas Eve is not a holiday in radio. I have to work and would be on air during my usual afternoon time slot, then have to drive home, feed the crew, etc. I wouldn't make it over to my sister's until 7:30–8 p.m.

By this time everyone would be ninety drinks into the festivities. Walking into a get-together in full swing, once in the door I was encouraged to fix myself a plate. Standing alone in her kitchen eating over her sink while everyone else was yukking it up felt half-rotten to me.

I knew that I had to make some changes and create a new tradition for myself—and that meant I wanted to spend Christmas alone in New York City. It's a place I'm comfortable, stimulated, and completely anonymous. That choice felt liberating and totally my own.

Is it even possible to choose the life you want to live? How much say do we get in it?

The life I want is far from perfect. Perfect is predictable and uninteresting to me. It's also unattainable, so let that go. Too many outside shitstorms will try and get in the way. But at least having the imagined blueprint for your life and practices is a mercurial and wonderful thing.

We can choose how we react to monkey wrenches thrown into our chosen life. Living life isn't an exact science, as we all know; we're emotional and vulnerable and flawed, thank god. So there is nothing more frustrating than catching yourself reacting in a way you don't like. On the other hand, it's got to be a valuable lesson to see what our authentic selves do when cornered by adversity. To live engaged in the world *now,* as it is.

How can we use life's random disappointments while maintaining the integrity we know we are capable of? Inherent genetic predispositions aside, does this imply we are too passive or limited to redirect where we want our lives to be? Are we too afraid to even envision what that could look like?

Circumstances and some wonky, ill-thought-out decisions have certainly affected my imagined life. I work on trying to accept those things and not let them define who I am, ultimately. I'll stick that crap in my toolbox, as it will surely come in handy.

THERE WERE QUITE A FEW raised eyebrows when I told people of my new plans. I realize that you are expected to gather up with family and friends and partake in certain rituals, and the idea of roaming the streets on Christmas Day alone, drinking a coffee across the street from the Dakota Building (I have never walked on the side of the street where the entrance is located—hallowed ground to me), then going to a Holocaust movie is not everyone's idea of 'Tis the Season. But it feeds my soul in a way that no holi-dazed jive would ever come close to doing.

You say "Christopher," I say, "Walking."

My standard answer to anyone's inquiry of "How far is that?" I say it's all within walking distance.

That is what I do when in the Big Apple. I have my routine spots I like to hit up: I always walk past the apartment building that I lived in and look up at the window where my younger self looked out at a very uncertain time in my life. Then the best part . . . I walk away.

My favorite city of romance and ghosts. I love being asked for directions by tourists. Wandering into a teenybop clothing store with hideous Top 40 blaring with no other intention than looking at others who feel at home in these joints.

Walking the streets at ass-kicking speed; if something catches your interest you investigate without hesitation. Knowing there is nowhere I have to be and nothing I have to do is the most liberating feeling imaginable, and I'm not the type to find that solace on some faraway beach. Nothing is more nourishing than eating a chopped salad bought at the corner deli and watching a marathon of *Long Island Medium* in my hotel room on Christmas Eve. I think what I like so much is the fact that you are completely aware of a huge city's occupants all participating in things you have no interest in, and nobody expects you to engage. There is no judgment; just comfort in knowing what is not for me.

My macabre fixation on watching local newscasts is especially fascinating because every story is like a headline ripped from the *National Enquirer.* A Queens man dressed as Santa Claus lit himself on fire and ran through the children's ward of the Flushing Medical Center. This ain't even the lead story. In Minneapolis the local news headline is, See how one MN man taught his pet squirrel to water-ski!

My December trip to NYC has become my thing. The people in my life have accepted that this is where I'll be. I'm not saying they understand it, but they've stopped fighting it.

And just like putting up a Christmas tree and lights I have my own set of rituals.

I buy a coffeemaker for my room, lay down cash for a nice-smelling candle and bath products. Purchase a bouquet of Stargazer lilies. I rearrange the lighting in the hotel. Engage the Do Not Disturb light. I then follow every whim I have alone. I am not a visitor; this is where I'm living.

Also a few times throughout the year I go back to NYC, the real city that feels like home. Absorbing everything and everyone, finding inspiration is easy. I don't go to live shows and rarely meet up with friends. Though everyone I do know lives within six blocks of each other off Avenue A in the East Village.

Years ago, I was interviewing Margaret Glaspy, who had recently moved to New York City. I had to restrain myself from kicking her in the shin when she complained about lack of inspiration in her new chosen city. Say what now? That response was inconceivable to me, and personally insulting, but I'll chalk it up to her having an off day. Or maybe she's never once left her apartment.

I've got my books, capable pet sitters, an open window to smoke by, and a beautifully dirty view. I have interesting faces to look at in passing; I can imagine their whole life story if I get a good enough glimpse. I talk to strangers void of small talk, and they stay with me in a way that I hold on to.

I have a certainty that I will do this for the rest of my life.

To be alone with everybody is the best gift I've ever given myself.

19

TAKING A LEAVE OF ABSENCE FROM WORK AND MY MIND

THIS NIGHTMARE JIG IS UP. TIME TO GO PUBLIC WITH ALL THAT I HAD been dealing with silently for two years. The fleeing my house in the night to stay at some crummy hotel. Why I had refrained from the usual public appearances.

Making a public statement to my listeners and the local media explaining the reason for taking a short leave from my job that I loved.

Duck and cover.

It was the end of March, and I was closing out my afternoon show. I had nothing rehearsed to say, so when the last song faded out, I carefully said, "I'm taking some time off to deal with a stalker that has been wreaking havoc in my life for a long time. Upcoming trial and sentencing dates, etc. I can't wait to return to the job I love when this is over."

Little did I know how empty the reality of this being truly over would be.

I didn't elaborate, but finally uttering the word *stalker* aloud felt like I had pulled the pin on a grenade. Now his arrest and warrants were public information so any local news reporter could look it up if they wanted to further elaborate.

Particularly his first mug shot photo, which was splashed all over the news. I never wanted to look closely and examine the details of his face, besides resembling Jabba the Hutt, which seemed a source of humor to some. I guess if he resembled Sam Shepard, it would seem less sleazy.

The disconnect between what I'd been put through by this blank face who, moving forward, would forever be linked to my name in a simple Google search just made me feel ill.

THIS BECAME its own challenge in that the media that covered my case seemed only to report the stalker as sending flowers or some other innocuous item. Perhaps it was lazy reporting, but it minimized the creepiness of what he did actually deliver to my doorstep.

My frustration at the downplaying of his pursuit was something I had to accept, knowing that one day in court I would be able to reveal the truth.

In hindsight unwanted is unwanted: it doesn't matter whether he secretly paid off my student loans or left a severed head on my stoop—it's all an invasion. Anybody who tries to quantify what constitutes threatening is missing the point.

It's utterly chilling to be holding in your hands a letter from someone you don't know talking about your wet pussy. Just having these letters in my possession made me sick.

You can only compartmentalize these things to a degree.

You have to live your life despite this. Things need your attention at home, your car needs repair or whatever. Walking into a gas station, I felt like this was written all over my face. Act normal. They don't care that you're being hunted. Pay for the gas and leave.

I HIRED A TREE TRIMMER to consult my situation of dead branches in my yard. Upon arrival the man walked through my gate and blurted out before any formal greeting, "I know who you are!"

Looking me up and down he offered, "What are you, a buck fifteen?" which like a carny I realized he was guessing my body weight. Before I could process any of this encounter, he said that he had read I have a stalker and launched into a preposterous hard sell on why I should own a firearm. I'm not kidding. Not one word had been mentioned about my trees. Straight into gun talk. I was so thrown and uncomfortable with his love affair of owning a piece and his conviction that I couldn't possibly defend myself without one, we never even got to the estimate portion of why he was there in the first place. I couldn't wait to get him out of my yard.

I told my brother about this random encounter, and he offered to come over to help me with my dead branches. Showing up on his bike not in possession of any tree-trimming tools. He impulsively began shimmying up the trees like a monkey. His well-thought-out idea was to simply hang from the dead branches until they broke off.

Immediately, my internal Google map was trying to figure which hospital emergency room was closest. I tried to get him to see the unnecessary danger he was putting himself in.

"Do you want it to look like someone lives here or not?" was his only argument as he moved onto another dead branch and swung like a gymnast in Converse low-tops.

Sleep patterns were altered in a way that had me running on fumes most days. It took a while before I realized I would lay in bed trying to fall asleep with tightly clenched fists. It might seem like a meaningless detail, but it felt as though I was ready to do battle cold-cocking any sound in the darkness. My dreams had become sweat-soaked-sheet scenarios of fighting off a faceless unknown force that wanted to do me damage. My eyes would open, and I would suck air as if I'd been underwater for a few hours. Now I was up. Didn't matter what time it was, or how much actual sleep I got. Laying back down with eyes closed, my nightmares picked up exactly where they left off. Simply pressing pause on the consuming threat of my unconscious.

Dreams of whimsy had been replaced with fitful trances, the feeling of falling, or throwing a punch underwater.

I looked like Pacino in *The Godfather Part III*. My eye bags had baggage. I felt hideous. I drank so much water I landed in the ER. Apparently, you can drink too much water: did you know that?

My usual was three one-liter bottles of Smart water a day.

On Labor Day for the first and only time in my life I thought I might faint. I didn't feel confident to drive, and nobody was around on the holiday, so I called a cab to go to the hospital. I actually sprawled out in the back seat of the taxi trying to offer directions to the driver on how best to find the ER entrance.

Upon arrival, I learned that any mention of having trouble breathing you skip to the front of the queue. In a matter of minutes, I was hooked up to a heart monitor and had a chest X-ray.

I was robbed of all electrolytes and potassium and whatever else you need to be upright. The attending physician trying to find a vein to start an IV saw my scars on my arms and casually asked if I worked at a pizza restaurant. "What would account for those scars?" he quizzically asked no one in particular. I knew he knew, but I didn't feel up to discussing my life as a cutter.

He hedged around with some obvious questions about stress levels and asked if this was my normal weight before finally fessing up to knowing who I was and had been aware of my present situation. I sat there feeling stupid and exposed that I had landed in the hospital for drinking too much water. Not eating. I had scars on my forearm. I was falling apart.

PRELIMINARY VISITS TO the courthouse to meet with my appointed attorney, Khaki Dockers, and the Victims' Rights advocate (a righteous boss named Linda) occurred weekly before the scheduled first hearing.

I wear at least four pounds of solid silver jewelry that I never take off except at airports. Realizing all of my body would be walking through a metal detector each time we entered the courthouse government building, it became this bizarre ritual to remove all of it.

Instead of leaving it at home, I would pack it in a see-through Ziploc freezer bag and then once through security I felt I had to put all of it back on before meeting with the lawyer. It had really become like armor, and oh how I love my brother and my dear friend Abbie who never questioned the absurdity of why I felt the need to make them wait while I reapplied every last bracelet.

I KNOW I'M PAINTING with a wide brush when I say that women were unequivocally more helpful on every level of this ordeal than men. The court-appointed prosecutor wasn't the most likable fellow, not that we needed to be chums; in fact, the joke is you should always hire an attorney or a talent agent that you personally can't stand. That way you can rest assured they will be distastefully aggressive and get the job done on your behalf.

I immediately asked if he'd ever handled a case of stalking. Predictably he said he hadn't.

No matter his litigious prowess: I felt defeated thinking I had to roll out my entire story in full to yet another stranger. *When would this end?* I began to think of my case as a telemarketer selling a bag of shit. With the omnipresent feeling I had best hawk it in order to be understood.

At some point while waiting for a court date, he introduced the idea of accepting a plea deal. If unfamiliar, the short version is settle this out of court. The expense of a trial is nothing anyone wants or advocates for. I interpreted it all as let it drop and move on. Moving ahead judicially felt like my only option, and anything less seemed to undermine the severity of this crime once again.

I didn't feel like I was putting anyone out by proceeding as planned. I should have realized it was a foreshadowing of the process: someone convince this hysterical woman that she's wasting time and resources by wanting accountability.

Plenty of times I hesitated to challenge him with "Has anyone ever threatened to rape you or kill your dogs? Would you agree to a plea deal if this was happening to your wife or daughter?"

So many of Shit Bag's ugly threats were embarrassing to repeat to a stranger, let alone my family.

20

WHAT'S YOUR PAIN LEVEL AT?

I'VE BEEN HOSPITALIZED FOR SOME GNARLY AND PAINFUL SURGERIES these past few years.

Two things I find problematic.

One: having more than one In Case of Emergency contact to list in my chart. No one I know picks up their ringing phone. Also, just for fun, for many years I listed an ex-boyfriend who'd done me dirty as my emergency contact, knowing I would derive some satisfaction if he were called in the middle of the night to identify my headless body at the morgue.

Two: the dreaded intake question "What's your pain level at?"

I have a wicked threshold for physical pain and feel that the distorted "worst pain possible" face at level 10 must be reserved for those who have a hacksaw lodged in their eye. Growing up with the parental attitude of "I don't care if you've severed your spinal cord, you're GOING to school tomorrow," I developed a shake-it-off anti-hypochondriac normalization of physical pain.

A few years ago, I found myself in agony one night. My go-to mystery diagnosis is usually food poisoning. However, I felt like I was being sawed in half with a dull letter opener, not that I'd consumed bad romaine. I found out later that my appendix had apparently exploded like a dirty bomb, but when I checked into the emergency room and was asked for my pain level, 8 was as high as I was willing to reveal.

Believing that I was dying, I found the perfunctory pregnancy test annoying. Chop, chop! Like it or not, if I'm croaking, I'm taking everyone down with me. Next came the required drinking of a gallon of barium dye, which tastes like artificial fruit and antifungal foot medicine. Good luck keeping it down.

Once you're out of all the scans and removed from imaging coffins, you are finally admitted into a hospital room, where you have a dry-erase board on the wall for nurses to keep track of med administration, their personal grocery lists, and the name of the current nurse on duty.

Self-projecting that all underpaid attending nurses hate their jobs, I felt compelled to make friendly small talk each time they came into my room. I found myself asking a pregnant nurse detailed questions about her upcoming baby shower—*Lord, who am I?*—when all I really wanted to do was rip the drugs out of her hands and self-administer.

Waking up after one of those twelve-minute fitful sleep windows you're allowed, I looked up at the board and saw, written beneath my name, the words *stoic patient*.

This was puzzling. I maybe had my own definition of the word *stoic* and wondered how someone had reduced me to these words. I asked the attending physician why I was considered stoic and who had made that personality assessment.

The short answer I received was, "You're low-key and quiet and don't yell at people. Your tone and facial expressions don't match up with the severity of what's happening in your body." HUH?

That's just being polite, isn't it? Who wants to be yelled at? So if I started throwing bedpans, leaning on the call button, and cursing out nurses for stronger pain meds, would that be preferable?

Again, with my feelings of pure projection, these people probably hate their jobs most nights and patients acting out is so commonplace it's surely exhausting. So I'm thinking that even if I'm at a pain level where I've begun to hallucinate a conversation with Helen Keller, why make it their problem?

Hmmm . . . I wonder where I learned this. Why at pain level eleventy million do I feel it's my job to make the attending medical staff feel comfortable and amused? It's amazing how quickly I become a performing chimp. Once the sweet, sexy Dilaudid hits my bloodstream, I invariably start my nightclub act. *Let's have some laughs while we're here. You've been a great audience!*

While being rolled down the hall, I mentioned to the orderly that it might be funny to paint the recovery room ceiling in a satanic fresco of flames and devils to resemble hell. He didn't get it and ignored me. I still insist this is a missed opportunity to make people's hospital experience more fun.

Once in the operating room, I remembered I hadn't taken out my belly ring. By their reaction, I think this might've been the most complicated part of their procedure. Looking as though they'd never seen a piercing before, they began haphazardly yanking on it, which went nowhere until I suggested they cut it off. I mean, they've got the cutting tools handy and all. Understand, this is where my absurd need to entertain and assist everyone finally ends.

Next stop, my favorite hospital experience: the magic of anesthesia.

I may be the only person who has zero fear of being put under. Everyone with their What if I never wake up? jive. Are you kidding? That'd be ideal! Takes a lot of pressure off me. It's the best sleep I'll ever have! Also, guess who's not paying this exorbitant hospital bill? *Me*! Simply count backward and die.

While in the recovery room somewhere between awake and floating toward the tunnel of light, the anesthesiologist came by my bed to tell me what a great singer his niece was and that I should check out her stuff on Bandcamp.

My eyes weren't even open. I couldn't have formed a sentence with a gun to my head. This would've been the perfect opportunity to become something other than Stoic Patient.

Is it too much to ask that you stick to your job of keeping me breathing before you hit me up about your *American Idol* reject niece's band?

Level 10 all the way.

21
HIGHWAY 61 REGURGITATED

MEMPHIS WAS ONE OF THE CITIES I HAD CONSIDERED STARTING A NEW life in. Naturally, when I had my first chance to come up for air, this is the city I needed to explore with a proper road trip.

Every time I told someone I was taking my first trip to Memphis, I was met with "What? You've never been??" Seems almost criminal that you can call yourself a music history fan and not already made the trip to Mecca via Highway 61.

I've done quite a bit of traveling, and never have I gotten so many tips on what to do. Everyone seems to know the very best place to get blackened catfish, where the cleanest truck stop restrooms are, and what legendary musical must-sees I had to add to my list.

Taking the longer and more scenic route of driving along the Mississippi River, I saw my first eagle. I know, shut up. Keep in mind, I get jazzed seeing a hoodrat bunny in Uptown. Making a stop in Arkansas, I found myself chatting with a huge amount of very friendly natives. One woman manning a tourism desk at a roadside stop asked me if my tattoo was a bobcat. I told her no, it was Satchmo who was a Maine Coon, so while large, she was not a feral wild animal. Marlene proceeded to tell me in great detail about how she raised a wild bobcat who slept on top of the fridge, and all was good until the neighbors' pit bull got after him, and her husband had to beat the dog with a bird feeder pole. They brought the bobcat—who

I'll call Lester—to the vet, and the vet clinic burned down. I tried as hard as I could to act like I'd heard stories like this all the time. Damn Yankee. But I quickly noticed that no matter how janky the interaction, everyone was sincerely polite.

First night in Memphis was mostly wandering downtown lighting other people's smokes (my Rick Steves travel tip is if you want to make friends in the South, get a lighter). Beale Street was a corny tourist trap; try as I may, I had no interest in kicking it in the Hard Rock Cafe–styled BB King's restaurant. No matter, I had plenty on tap for the next day: I had to figure out what to wear to Graceland.

Driving down Elvis Presley Boulevard was everything it should be: seedy and swarming with Ed and Betty's. Parking next to nine hundred RVs with every state represented in license plates only built my anticipation. I've heard a ton about Graceland—people describing the rooms in detail—but knowing that I would see with my own eyes the green-carpeted walls and ceramic monkeys and abundance of RCA TV sets was a kick. Oddly knowing that Sam Phillips had sold the king's contract to RCA for chump change made it all the crazier that Graceland was filled with "gift TV sets": Thanks, Elvis. You sold eight million records for us this month, so here's a free TV set, which by the way, you paid for. Thank you, ladies and gentleman. Thank you very much.

Nerd alert: I had to Google Elvis's height, because at 5'6", I nearly clocked my head into several low ceilings—granted, they were all plushily carpeted. How did 'Cilla's beehive make it through the Arabian Nights Billiard Room entryway? I kept my snark to myself every time the joint was referred to as "The Mansion"; I thought without the racketball court, and the horse farm, it would probably go for $248,900 in Minneapolis. Hell, throw in the makeshift indoor shooting range and they could fetch another C-note. I stood alongside everyone soaking in all its decor with utter reverence. If Mike Brady had designed the Sistine Chapel perhaps.

I was indeed well received at Graceland.

Next stop, Stax Records. A steamy 98 degrees outside. Sitting down in the air-conditioned theater to watch the short Stax documentary, I got chills just seeing the iconic finger-snap logo onscreen. Various Stax artists talked about the history of the label, spelling out clearly that they did not share the same intentions as Motown. They knew who their audience was. The roster was racially integrated, and many women played pivotal roles. Gospel, soul, and country. Got it? Good. Walking through the brilliantly curated museum was jaw dropping. Oh, hi, Booker T's organ he used on the recording of *Green Onions*—you look so nice just a few steps away from Isaac Hayes's actual Cadillac, complete with funked-up fun fur interior. He's a bad mutha. Shut your mouth.

A series of Terry Manning's photographs on display included possibly the coolest shots ever of Chuck Berry and of Big Star's Chris Bell. As I exited the gift shop with my bags filled with Stax swag, I knew this was an experience I would hold on to for a long time.

The next day's agenda was the Civil Rights Museum, which is built off of the Lorraine Hotel where Dr. Martin Luther King Jr. was assassinated. Powerful stuff looking up at the balcony outside of room 306 where he last stood. The weight of this historical site didn't feel right to snap selfies in front of. Inside, the thoughtfully curated museum held our nation's history, brutal and many times hard to look at and fully absorb. Yet there was a real spirit within these walls: one of suffering and fighting for basic human rights, acts of courage and tenacity. I loved the huge number of children who were taking this tour, and I tried to imagine how they were taking all of this in. You could easily spend hours here. Embarrassing side note: I nearly heaved going through security realizing I carry a switchblade with me in my purse. Please, Civil Rights Museum lady, don't boot me for carrying the single most inappropriate item into the most sacred of places. I told her she had pretty hair and that seemed to distract her while lightly looking into my purse.

Switching gears, I was off to Sun Studio. I kept likening a lot of this experience to when people meet Tom Cruise in person and remark, "He seems so much bigger in the movies; he's just a little guy." That only adds to the wonder that this music was created in tiny spaces, yet everything about it was HUGE. Sam Phillips was looking for a sound yet to be identified as rock and roll proper—get your head around that. Howlin' Wolf, the Prisonaires (a band of actual inmates that had to be accompanied by armed guards), Ike Turner, and Elvis Presley all stood here at one time, all hoping to make something happen with their music. In the case of Jerry Lee Lewis, he didn't come to the studio with a well-produced demo tape in hand; rather, traveling up with his daddy asking if there was a piano he could play seems unreal. Man, I'm glad he did.

Huddled in Sun's recording studio, looking at the vintage gear and photos of Johnny Cash, Carl Perkins, Jerry Lee, and Elvis, again my mind drifted to what the room must've felt like with all of that talent assembled at one time. What did it smell like? Who in the room was packing speed or heat? I'd wager all of them.

At the end of the tour, we shuffled out and asked Jason, our tour guide, questions. Lamely, all I could come up with was, "Were there any restrictions to the imbibing of alcohol during recording sessions?"

"It was liberal," was the honest answer.

Still buzzing from Sun Studio and walking down the railroad tracks along the Mississippi River, I got my first look at a magnolia tree. Splendid. It was also noteworthy that on several occasions I noticed random acts of kindness on the streets. People coming out of delis with a bag of food and giving it to someone who looked like they really needed it. People noticing those who go unnoticed and treating them with dignity.

Next day was to see Ardent Studios, a still-working studio; in fact, on that day I heard someone playing a piano in one of the studios with an open door. It was Greg Dulli. Knowing that the members of Big Star all had copies of the key to let themselves in to record whatever drunken jam in the middle of the night made me want to rewatch the Big Star documentary. Ardent, like everything in Memphis, is preserved. No fancy upgrading. If there was a shitty plaid sofa in the control room in 1974, it is still there and you are looking at it, son.

A huge thrill was to get a private tour of Sam Phillips's office, led by his nephew, Jud, who was possibly one of the friendliest guys I've ever met. Again, this place was small, small, small. It smelled a bit aquatic as if it had been underwater for a decade or two. The reception area had two groovy chairs and a small desk. There was the perfectly intact bar with gnarly wallpaper. Can you imagine who might've sat on one of those stools knocking back a Coca-Cola and negotiating a contract? Jud Phillips casually asked us if we knew Jack White. Turns out Jack had just picked up the reception-area sofa to reupholster. Why not?

Inside Sam's office was a trip. Was it in here that Sam contemplated selling Elvis's contract? Good thing he did, as it kept the studio afloat to go on to work with a myriad of legends. Lesson learned. Take a risk in life, why dontcha.

The Peabody Hotel was the next stop, where the plan was to sit in the grand lobby and watch the Changing of the Ducks. Twice a day, the lobby fills with hundreds of people to see five ducks walk out of an elevator and scamper into the fountain, then at 5 p.m., with much pomp and flair, they are led back to their suite where I imagine they order room service and rest with cucumbers on their eyes in little white-towel turbans.

Lansky's has a store in the hotel; it was Elvis's official clothier for some time. On the wall were a few signed photos and a guitar signed by Steve Jones and John Lydon of the Sex Pistols. Connecting the dots from England's premier punk band to Memphis was further explained that Rambo—John Lydon's friend/roadie/overseer of all things Rotten—got married at the Peabody, where Johnny served as best man. Now I really want to know what he wore.

The trip was flawless. If there was any regret, it was that I found out last minute that Jerry Lee Lewis was having a yard sale the next day. Not an estate sale, but a yard sale. It wasn't going to be diamond-encrusted pianos and silk smoking jackets for sale. Immediately,

I fantasized about owning one of the Killer's ashtrays or Garden Weasels. It was about a half-hour out of Memphis, and I didn't have the time, but just to have done a drive-by shouting out the car window at no one in particular, "How much you want for the Lawn Jarts?" would've sealed the deal of all of my rock and roll dreams.

Looch has left the building.

22
HALITOSIS

FIRST THING THAT SHOULD BE SAID ABOUT HAL IS THAT NO ONE called him "Dad." He didn't want to identify as a father in a traditional sense, which never seemed anything but perfectly normal to me.

I've since wondered if Hal had been alive during all this personal upheaval what he would've said to me. He wasn't involved in any of his kids' lives overtly, he was mostly absent, but he wasn't unkind. He might have even said something funny.

After his passing so many people told me that they were sure he was looking out for me.

Which sadly I find funny. He didn't do that in his waking life—why now that he was gone would he suddenly be an angelic guardian and protector?

Death is really all about the living.

IN MY LIFE of selective spirituality, I've wrestled with any meaningful concept of the hereafter. I've known way too many people who've died, and with each person's passing the finality is startling. They're gone.

I once asked one of my brothers why he didn't visit Hal's grave, and he replied, "He's not there."

I understand the idea of keeping someone's "spirit" alive by telling stories and sharing experiences about the dearly departed. I'm down with that. In fact, before you jump down my agnostic throat, whatever gets you through the night is all right with me.

If the deceased were lucky enough to leave behind a body of work that can be read, listened to, or watched, it might make the process infinitely more accessible. But let's be real: not everyone we have loved and lost was a poet or singular performer. I've known plenty of crumbums whose limited contributions to the world wouldn't elicit a subpar tribute band—or even a decent eulogy, for that matter.

Firsthand experience has shown me we selfishly expect comfort from the dying. Does that seem fair? Don't they have enough on their plate with the whole impending dust-to-dust examination of all their earthly deeds? Maybe they aren't obligated to reassure us, the living, that their pain is manageable, they have no problem letting go, and that they see angels with welcoming arms?

The whole idea of understanding how death is *supposed* to go down is ludicrous. I never got the user manual on what to expect when one is croaking. My feeling is you can't really say or do anything wrong. I accept death will remain a mystery I will stay curious for.

The only possible people who might have perused this mythical manual are hospice workers. These are the real-Earth angels. I marvel at their abilities and intuition. This is a job I could never be qualified for. (A close second is rodeo clown—I couldn't do that gig either.)

Those who lean into religion have a clear advantage over we heathens. Visions of a well-conceived paradise, along with a reunion of family and friends. Here is where the believers might have a bit of cherry-picking selectivity: to believe one is only reunited with well-loved family and cherished old friends. My ghoulish concern is my heavenly homecoming might be with my old sketchy piano teacher or some slumlord who denied me my damage deposit or the hostile English teacher who handed back my writing assignments with loud red ink in the margins simply stating AWK. As in awkward. Who also told me in front of the whole class that I don't write well because it sounds too much like the way I talk. To which I say today, "Go scratch."

Try sitting at your own father's deathbed, who makes no mention of inner peace, heaven, or his personal savior. Instead, he talks only of the Grim Reaper hiding in the shadows of his room, personal regrets, and realized shortcomings about how much he fucked up in life.

Did I suddenly drop to my knees and begin praying? I did not. I listened. I answered his morphine ramblings with a simple, "It's okay." Because, at that point, doesn't it have to be?

Does anyone really expect that this is the perfect time to throw down and rehash the past, point by point, airing grievances and demanding apologies? Death is so embarrassingly intimate. Everything around it is minimized to small gestures. Whispering, hand-holding, reading quietly in an uncomfortable chair.

The last lucid conversation I had with Hal, he was cussing me out as I tried to remove his compression socks. Which is par for the course and makes me laugh to this day. Just because he was dying didn't mean he would adopt a new saintly personality and way of being. It was authentic, and I've come to appreciate the honesty.

LOOPING BACK to the idea of keeping someone's spirit alive: I know I do that.

He's in my DNA. His eccentricities always make their way into my storytelling. I'll tell you one of my favorite things about him that'll kick up some immortal dust: every time he sneezed—and think of how many times a person sneezes in their entire life—he'd wrinkle his nose pre-sneeze and then cover his mouth and yell, GODDAMNIT!! into his hand. EVERY SINGLE TIME. I must've heard that a million times over the course of my life.

He also was a man who could swim with a lit cigar in his mouth.

I treasure his throwaway comments, which were daily. When coming downstairs before high school he would ask if I'd combed my hair with a live chicken. Standing in front of the microwave yelling, "COME ON!!"

Reading the newspaper at the kitchen table, he'd ask what I had done the night before, responding that I'd used a fake ID to see the Bad Brains. His half-response over the paper was "Atta girl."

This is the man who would toast bread for the birds in the winter ensuring they received a hot meal. My soft heart for animals was cemented early.

NOW IT'S MY TURN to cherry-pick: the one exception I make on my beliefs of life after death is with animals. All of our pets go to heaven. With hearts so pure, it only makes sense there would be a reserved place of warmth and unconditional love—an extension of what our fur babies gave to us, without question—with the added benefit of invisible poop. Nothing but open spaces and comfortable sleeping spots. It also smells fantastic, like Aveda products and clean sheets.

I'm still trying to evolve my piecemeal idea of life after death. For now, I'm sticking with the hope that I might be able to visit this magical place and hold every dog and cat I've ever loved, stroking their velvety ears if even just for one day.

SAYING GOODBYE to Hal felt like an official end.

On the gray November day after he shuffled off to the great Dean Martin Roast in the sky, I was sitting in my second-floor apartment looking out at the bare tree branches.

The image of his frail deathbed was so fresh I was willing my mind to remember him before his sickness.

Late 1970s Hal, giving me a buck on his bike after dinner to pick up a pack of Kool's.

Catcher's mitt complexion, permanently darkened by his worship of the sun. Thick black hair and small frame sitting at the yellow Formica kitchen booth table reading the paper.

In this moment of intent reflection, a giant bright red male cardinal settled as close as a bird could land without flying directly into the pane of glass.

Without directly summoning him, I knew this was forever to be my sign.

Hard to explain, so I don't.

Cardinals are quite common year-round in Minneapolis. But the consistency with which my thoughts of Hal are accented by a sudden red bird sighting is staggering.

I've even gotten cocky and told a few people that I could summon him on command. I crap you negative; he shows up. Like a spiritual party trick.

Only it's downright sacred to me.

While cooking your recipe for sausage and peppers in the backyard: you came to visit.

I will never take this for granted. It's always lovely to see you, Hal.

If somewhere in the distance, I hear GODDAMNIT! I'll believe we all have a chance in hell to be in heaven.

23

SHINGLES AT THE STONES

Finally having found a new shrink, our sessions started the day after my leave of absence from work began.

While sitting in the waiting room for my first appointment with Belinda, someone was holding the daily newspaper up in front of their face. There I was in black and white: the local news had broken the story about my stalker. There was also his big fat mug shot as well.

This would've been funny if it was happening to someone else. I was momentarily concerned that the paper used an old photo of me wearing a stupid beret. I let it slide.

> **News from KARE 11**
> **CRIME**
> **Author: Dana Thiede and Jana Shortal and KARE**
> **April 9, 2015**
>
> MINNEAPOLIS—A man accused of stalking a popular Twin Cities Radio personality is set to go on trial Tuesday.
>
> Court documents reflect the felony stalking charges Hennepin County prosecutors have filed against 56-year-old Patrick Henry Kelly of Eden Prairie. In the criminal complaint filed against Kelly prosecutors allege that the defendant violated a harassment

restraining order filed against him by Mary Lucia, a well-known radio host on 89.3 The Current.

Investigators chronicled at least five separate violations of the order between Aug. 12 and Oct. 21, 2014. It prohibited Kelly from being within two city blocks or a quarter mile from Lucia's home in all directions. The defendant allegedly left letters and gifts that included candles, a bottle of wine and flowers on her doorstep.

Lucia also told police she received a handwritten card in the mail, with handwriting she identified as Kelly's. The card stated "I wake up thinking of you and repeat before bed. This feeling is so real to me! Just can't ignore it anymore."

Prosecutors say harassment of Lucia actually traces back to February of 2014, when Kelly began sending unwanted letters and gifts, and started phoning and leaving voicemails for the DJ. Her employer sent him a letter instructing him to stop sending things as it was a violation of company policy. Kelly allegedly responded by email, saying he would stop trying to contact Lucia, but then began sending things to her personal address and cell phone.

In July, after the order of protection had been issued but before it had been served to Kelly, Minneapolis Police were called to Lucia's home after the defendant reportedly showed up on her doorstep with flowers and rang the doorbell for five minutes straight. Kelly left before officers arrived, but Lucia was able to identify him in a photo lineup.

Lucia detailed her ordeal in a letter she posted on The Current's website. In the letter, she informed listeners that she was taking a leave of absence due to the stress that the stalking had inflicted on her life. Lucia told authorities she felt terrorized by the defendant's escalating behavior, and said the repeated conduct has triggered intense stress, weight loss and has made it hard to concentrate and perform her job.

It's something Rana Alexander, a legal advocate for women in Lucia's situation, says should be brought out in the open.

> "There have been so many incidents that have not been talked about and I think it's important that we talk about it, it's been going on a long time, and no one has been saying anything," Alexander said broadly when speaking about women being stalked or harassed just because they are in the public eye.
>
> Lucia remains on leave from her position at The Current but said in her letter yesterday she plans to come back once this is behind her.

For a new patient there are twenty-five forms to fill out about yourself.

FUN.

The "Do I feel like committing suicide: Sometimes, Daily, Almost Never" questionnaire. I'm uncertain they ever read through my answers because they would've had the butterfly net waiting at my next appointment if they did.

STARTING OVER with a new therapist is daunting. How many dead bodies did I need to drag up?

I was in crisis with an impending court date on the books, and I wanted to talk with her about my current situation only. She was smart and resembled a more bohemian Hillary Clinton.

The minute I sat down in my chair, I felt an itch on my lower back.

I gave her the CliffsNotes version for her initial intake of me as a new patient. My skin felt like it was on fire. Had I been bitten by an insect in the lobby?

After about twenty minutes she inquired about my indiscreet twisting and scratching. I told her I might have a bug bite.

She asked to see my back. I lifted my T-shirt to reveal where a tramp stamp would be if I had one. Her reaction was swift. Her immediate diagnosis of shingles had me leaving her office and entering the other part of the clinic. My primary physician was also located in this building.

I sat waiting for her to see me, trying to get a glimpse in the small mirror of what the hell shingles looked like. All I could think was I've had barely twenty minutes talking to a new shrink before I'm being seen for a completely different issue.

When my doctor finally came in, again it was diagnosed in three seconds after lifting my shirt only slightly. Don't scratch it, I was told. She had to explain to me the whole chicken pox history jazz and then said it was also triggered by stress. Don't touch it directly, it could spread to your face. At this point I still hadn't gotten a look at what every other person was seeing.

She wrote a prescription for me and gave me the over/under on how long I would be affected.

If unfamiliar with this condition, it's not only the itchiest rash you can imagine, but it also affects the nervous system and hurts like a bitch and lastly, sweet Jehovah, it blisters.

Throw it on the pile!

I had exactly one minute and fifty-eight seconds left of the hour with my new shrink. I hustled back into her office and told her she had correctly diagnosed me from halfway across the room.

We set up another office visit in three weeks. Presuming the leprosy would be cleared up by then.

After getting the meds filled, I finally got home to take my first look at what was going on with my lower waist. What I thought to be a bug bite was the gnarliest reddest open-sored-looking nightmare. Great, this could spread to my face?

All I wanted to do was claw at my flesh. This fresh hell had moved to the front of my tummy just on one side.

I SAT IN A BATH of oatmeal that night chanting my Doofus Wainwright mantra I had recently concocted.

Power. Creativity. Peace.

More like Fuck, Fuck, Fuck.

I'd also been advised to photograph this as "evidence" of my stress. Lord, which lucky friend did I want to take a picture of me and my new disease? I had to create a folder in which to store all photos relating to the stalker. Shots of the garbage he left in my yard, unopened letters, and now my stomach.

The myriad of health problems that reared their head during this time nearly drove me crazy. I had been holding tickets for the Rolling Stones concert in June, never realizing when I purchased the tickets how fragile my health would be. I've said it many times: I wake up every day and think of the Stones, and I don't think there is anything odd about that. I was going no matter what.

My weight had dropped to 112 pounds, my hair had started falling out in clumps, I had hives. The inside of my mouth was bloody: I had developed a nervous habit of chewing the inside of my lips and cheeks. I attribute this to feeling silenced.

I planned to meet up with my two best mates from the station before the outdoor concert. It had been raining all day. My outfit choices were dictated by what I could tolerate against the angry blisters of shingles. I threw on an oversized rain poncho and took a Lyft to the stadium.

It was good to see the faces of my two work friends, one who was pregnant. I gave her an early baby shower Motorhead onesie, and we made our way to the soggy show. I didn't make eye contact with anyone. I hadn't been out in public for a few months. Our seats were wet bleachers. I tried not to think of what was happening under my rain getup, but every time I was bumped or jostled it felt like an electrocution.

Not much would keep me from seeing the Stones—not shingles, erectile disfunction, gout, crib death, or rain.

Suddenly faced with the idea of making my way home in a crowd of twenty thousand drunk concertgoers, I realized grabbing a Lyft or a taxi was not feasible. The light rail train station was near the stadium, which would get me halfway home. My rock buzz died quickly when I saw the line for the train platform. I had no choice: I got into the never-ending line and waited and waited. Three trains had filled to capacity before I even got to the boarding area. Once on the train it was sardine-packed and I stood near the door with my face pointed into the arm pit of the dude grabbing a strap from above. The stench of B.O., booze, and rain-soaked bodies was permeating my nostrils. I tried breathing through my mouth. Once the train was in motion, so were the unsteady loud passengers lurching about my half-inch of personal space. Under normal situations this would be slightly annoying, but with a raging case of shingles every elbow and backpack found its way with laser precision to my oozing blistered midsection. These tipsy clods had no way of knowing that if I had a knife on me, at least half the rowdy concertgoers would all be stabbed.

Don't you know the crime rate's going up, up, up, up, up? Shadoobie, shattered.

24

BRING ME DEAD FLOWERS

I RECEIVED AN EMAIL FROM A BRITISH FILM COMPANY ASKING IF THEY could talk to me about my case. I couldn't imagine that my story would've traveled across the pond and be of interest to anyone. I did a bit of research before responding, and they seemed legit. They had affiliations with National Geographic. I said that they could call me. I spoke with a producer who explained they were doing a series on stalking, documentary style.

I was intrigued enough to answer some questions. I also asked a lot of questions. The producer seemed thoughtful and informed. She began the pitch with a free trip to London, accommodations, and two days of required filming. In my head I was imagining an interview with myself and a national platform to express the frustrations of a legal system that perpetually bungled cases of felony stalking. I had even talked myself into thinking it could be cathartic to tell my story.

Not to mention the idea of traveling to another continent held alarming appeal. Maybe I'd stay and get a job for the BBC.

In a second phone interview her questions leaned more heavily into the perverted aspects of the case. Red flag #1. I get it. She wanted the dirty details to make something more compelling. That's when I asked if she had samples of their work that I could look at. She sent me a link to a fully produced episode.

Red flag #2: reenactments.

This was the cheesiest kind of television I despised. I was this close to falling for it because a free trip to London had been offered.

Immediately I messaged the producer backing out of any involvement, taking on the blame of misunderstanding that this was a dramatic reenactment show when I thought it was a straight interview documentary style.

I'd just have to hold on to my story longer.

It then became a source of comedy trying to imagine them "casting me" or, worse yet, HIM.

MY NEXT OBSESSION became scrutinizing over all of my past social media posts in which one of my dog or cat's ID collar was visible. You'd maybe never think of things like that, but when the realization that my phone number and address were printed on all of my babies' collar tags, I was on a twisted mission deleting innocent photos I had once been so proud to share with friends.

I had more than one woman reach out to me with a similar nightmare of being stalked and ask what advice could I offer them. One being a former radio host who was sent taxidermy by mail, god bless her. Other than feeling like a complete failure in pep talks, all I could rattle off was: restraining order, cameras at home, blocking social media accounts, and being your own advocate. Mentally I couldn't offer anything in the way of encouragement. I was just as lost. Firmly of the belief that nothing works, and no one can help you.

To all the people who reached out to me with their own story of being stalked: I am sincerely sorry I couldn't offer more help. I hope at the very least I validated your experience. I know how hard it is to have to retell it over and over again. I heard you. I'm sorry I was still broken.

Especially disheartening was the growing assumption that because I held a job as a public figure, I must've had endless resources and privilege. Access to top lawyers and inside information.

Nope. I was just your average peasant struggling to tread water.

A company that is so concerned with optics didn't seem to think it was important to get too involved with "my problem." Never an offer of legal counsel to navigate this mess. And trust me, if there is one group employed by them that makes bank, it's their lawyers. Any suggestion that I was in this mess because of my job was dismissed. I was maybe their highest-profile employee, which came in handy when asking for monetary contributions. I was publicly being humiliated and very much tied to their brand. While I understand that stalking can happen to anyone, if I had worked at Radio Shack and this happened, would I be left to my own wits to fight this? Maybe. It just felt gross that when it served them, they would trot me out in front to generate revenue with awards I had won over the years. I was the brand voice of the station from Day One, and my ratings were consistently high. I so want to refrain from using the phrase "the Franchise," but corny shit like that holds value in this business. I wasn't the Michael Jordan of the station. Maybe Scottie Pippen. Actually, scratch that. I relate more to Dennis Rodman, who once said, "I'd play basketball for free. It's the bullshit you got to pay me for."

MANY WELL-INTENDED FRIENDS asked if I meditated and might that not help with my stress levels.

In theory that sounds fantastic, but when every sense is cranked to 11, quieting your thoughts feels impossible and becoming tuned in to the rhythm of your breathing is a recipe for a panic attack.

Reading was the closest I came to thinking outside of my own primitive feelings. Losing myself in other people's stories was a lifeline.

Luckily, I have a friend who was the music editor of a newspaper with plenty of rock bios on hand. One day a box arrived filled with irresistible trash.

I consumed biographies like a fiend. I gravitated toward stories involving singular talent, mental breakdown, drug addiction, and reinvention of one's career. John Lydon, Chrissie Hynde, Kim Gordon,

Howard Hughes, Ace Frehley, Montgomery Clift, Jerry Lee Lewis, Etta James, Leonard Bernstein, Judy Garland.

Go figure.

To break up the day every morning I ritualistically walked a couple blocks and sat outside at a local coffee shop with my book.

It felt natural to be somewhere everyday other than my house. I didn't listen to the radio. I didn't want to hear what was happening in my absence.

A stranger had taken me out of the place I had felt most comfortable. My job. My career.

Adjusting to life waiting on the court system to set a trial date was maddening. It never felt like a break or anything close to a vacation. I mention that because someone actually asked me if I was enjoying my "summer vacation." It sounds like an innocuous inquiry, but I had the shingles scars, bandaged wrists, and bleeding inner mouth to suggest otherwise.

The sun on my skin, overhearing people's breakfast talk, petting someone's dog. I pretended I was invisible. Never trying to meet anyone's eye. Just look down at your book.

I looked upon the staff as friends.

Occasionally a passerby recognized me and stopped for a quick chat, which I didn't mind. Especially if they inquired about what I was reading.

This became a safe bubble for me. I'd nurse a latte for a few hours and make my way home.

On one occasion I turned my key in the lock and opened my door into my kitchen. I was immediately put on guard. At first glance my house appeared to have been ransacked. The kitchen had kibble dog food scattered on the floor. Things were tipped over. Something clearly went down in here.

As I cautiously looked around it dawned on me that Muse, my senior cat, had knocked a full Tupperware container of dog food off a shelf. I can imagine the contents were frantically being hoovered by two nervous Pugs. Water dishes were spilled, a pile of heave on the floor. Pictures seemed crooked on the walls. What the hell?

Had I been burglarized, did someone let a stray goat into my house?

I could only laugh at the crime scene. This had Muse's wicked sense of humor written all over it. One swift swipe of her paw and utter mayhem broke out while she probably retreated somewhere else in the house giggling. At age nineteen it's also worth noting I can safely estimate she's watched *Gimme Shelter* thirty-eight times in the course of her life. Fun fact.

WITH FREQUENCY I woke up feeling like Sylvia Plath and Ian Curtis's bastard lovechild.

When life overwhelms me taking away what inner power I think I might possess, you already know I have a history of self-medicating and self-harm.

Drinking and drugging seems fairly obvious as a temporary escape. But I've always thought I had more imagination than that.

Kicking cold turkey was clearly the dumbest and best thing I had ever done.

Today I'm seeking alternate ways of dealing.

One answer has been right in front of me the whole time: looking deeply into the eyes of one(s) you love. Oxytocin comes flooding through my brain like warm syrup.

Dogs have somehow hijacked this oxytocin bonding pathway, so that just by making eye contact or hugging my dogs and cats the urge to repeat any of my old tricks seems so embarrassingly selfish.

Here in front of me is an animal looking deeply into my eyes revealing their purity and unconditional love.

I will honor this gift and hold on to this feeling of Gratitude or Catitude. I believe in DOG as my higher power.

25

AT THIS TIME, WE BEGIN OUR PRIORITY BOARDING OF ALL CATS

PERHAPS AS A MEANS OF PRESERVING MY SANITY I STILL ALLOWED brain space for the kind of whimsical thinking of what I imagine my animals might do in imagined life scenarios outside of my home.

I talk about the love of my three pugs because they are ham sandwiches and have never met a camera they didn't like. It's a given.

But I also share my life with three extraordinary cats who see their canine brethren and raise them a decapitated mouse head in your bed. "Why didn't you say you worked for Corleone, Tom?"

Let me start with the grande dame of the household, Muse. Or as the vet tech with her beautiful accent calls her, Moose.

Life began for this warrior princess in a paper bag dumped in a parking lot at Mississippi Market. The night I rescued her and took her home I was terrified my other cats at the time would think she was a rodent, that's how tiny she was. But when you're born on the mean streets of St. Paul and cruelly cast aside, you'd better believe she was a formidable force from the jump. She has ruled every household I've kept with an iron paw.

When I think of my cats individually, I like to imagine where they would be on a commercial airplane flight. Muse would have some special pre-board status, jump the line before the crew, and be half-asleep reclined in first class with cucumbers on her eyes while the other two were still fumbling with their e-tickets at the gate.

Eventually boarding: Stax, my gentleman Tuxedo, would be in an overhead bin helping others stow their carry-on bags. People would offer him a tip for his assistance, which he would politely decline. He would also be the passenger thoughtful enough to offer his window seat to a screaming child. He would not hog the armrest or kick your seat. He would curl up in a tiny ball dreaming peacefully of volunteering at a women's shelter all the while smelling of waffles and fabric softener.

Ditch, my youngest rescue, would be relentlessly scratching at the cockpit door, predicated on guile and handsome good looks, and he'd eventually be allowed entrance and get to sit on the pilot's lap during takeoff.

Once airborne, Muse would be the entitled cringey passenger insisting she leave her seat during the beverage service. Not taking no for an answer, she would leap the cart to use an empty seat to pee. She would then turn around back to her luxury roomy suite and start this hassle all over again. If anyone attempts to pet her in this process, she would shoot over a withering look that says, *You may touch me with your eyes only.*

The initial thrill of sitting in the cockpit will have, by now, become boring for Ditch, and he will be scratching against the cockpit door to be let out. Throughout the flight, he will do this seventeen more times. Cue the frustrated pilot saying, "Come on, in or out?"

Stealthily slinking underneath the seats, he will make his way to the one travel bag that contains any morsel of food. The unsuspecting passenger won't notice anything until they see a floofy orange cat running down the aisle with a croissant in his mouth. Ditch will also randomly puke twice during the flight.

Eventually settling on the tray top of a snoozing traveler, he will delete the Word document on their open laptop and scurry away.

Before returning to paw at the cockpit door, he will find a hair tie and kick it the entire length of the aircraft for twenty minutes.

Muse, irrationally galled by the color and pattern of the shirt her across-the-aisle passenger is wearing, will ring her call bell incessantly demanding the offending eyesore be moved back to coach. While the flight attendant politely explains he cannot accommodate her wishes, she will demand more free champagne and an extra blanket, threatening to write a letter to the CEO of the airline.

Approaching descent, Stax awakens and offers to collect empty cups. Ditch, back in the cockpit, has charmed his way into assisting with the engagement of the landing gear, while Muse has unbuckled and is already using electronic devices to ensure she is met at the luggage carousel.

Both pilots, who have severe cat allergies, fight to adopt Ditch.

Stax, the last one off the plane, thanks the crew by name.

Muse hops on an elderly couple's Skycap, insisting they stop for Kahlua at the duty-free.

26

KEEP IN MIND THERE WILL BE PLENTY OF LISTENERS WHO'VE FORGOTTEN YOU

I WAS SCHEDULED TO RETURN TO WORK AFTER THE COURT HEARINGS, initially thought to be in April; however, dates had been pushed back and changed too many times to count. His reoffending and dodging arrest had been going on for months.

My employers were more than anxious for my return. On a beautiful early autumn afternoon, I was summoned to a meeting with Potsy, his boss, and a woman from HR who already had one foot out the door.

We agreed to meet up at my local coffee shop to discuss where the case was and, what I quickly realized, to give them a definite return-to-work date. I hadn't had any communication with management since my leave. Knowing that I was about to face the corporate firing squad whose real interest was getting their afternoon drive host back on air, I proceeded with a cautiously optimistic attitude.

Not having seen their faces all summer, my first reaction was one of genuine good feeling. They were familiar and we were meeting on my turf as opposed to a bland conference room. We took a table by the window where the blinding sun blew all details off each other's faces.

There may have been some unspoken alarm at my appearance, but it was quickly covered with small talk. Before I could really launch into the past few months of how I had been living and what a realistic return to on air would look like before the sentencing hearing, etc., Potsy jumped in to thoughtfully remind me that I should keep in mind there will be plenty of listeners who've forgotten me, as well as those who hadn't noticed my absence at all. Good icebreaker!

Did I need to remind him that I'd been a fixture in local radio for twenty-four years, including fifteen at my present position? I was the goddamn branding voice for the entire station from the beginning. Frankly, it was no secret to everyone on staff that he was yearning for my job and jealous that I had made my name in a music market he craved to belong to. For the program director to appoint himself as the temporary fill-in host in the prime-time position I held during my absence says everything.

No way in hell was this going to be the appropriate time for another one of his shaming, spirit-breaking pep talks. I glanced at both HR woman and Potsy's boss to see if they had *any* reaction to this demeaning opening statement of his. Nothing registered faintly of embarrassment.

By all means, if it strengthens your fragile male ego to think that four months off air with a very public case of stalking that kept my name in the news constitutes me starting from zero, I should be quaking with fear that my entire radio career has been erased.

Fuck it, someone change his diaper.

Some combination of the bureaucracy of short-term leave payment and my willingness to play ball had me agreeing to return to work with the case still pending. I did however stipulate I would only return Monday to Thursday. Friday was my mental health day; my nonnegotiable Skype shrink appointment and half-baked acupuncture sessions both had been reserved on Friday.

I had no idea how I would feel about making that daily drive into the station; it might sound overblown, but it felt like I was returning to a crime scene. I was still under the gag order of an upcoming court date. One thing I did advocate strongly for was to report to any manager that wasn't Potsy. Turned down flat. Other employees on air had different direct reports, so it wouldn't have been so earth-shattering for me to switch. Potsy's boss and outside-of-work Bro-ski wouldn't even entertain the idea. More interesting to me was that he made no inquiries about why I wanted this change.

My first day back to work, before taking the stairs to the fourth floor, I hightailed it down to the newsroom to seek out my pal Bob who I had done my daily 4:20 news break with for years.

Innately I knew if anyone in that building would understand my experience with as few words possible it would be Bob. He was at his desk, and I came up behind him quietly. He turned in his chair and we shared a hug. The kind of hug like the plane was going down hug. Certain people get you—sometimes it's really that simple. I know you. You know me.

I've been broken and I'm taking whatever steps to return to myself. Cue up Dorothy hugs the Scarecrow. See ya at 4:20!

I STARTED MY FIRST SHOW with Tom Petty's "I Won't Back Down."

Might seem corny but it meant everything to me. I had been accustomed to playing songs with pointed lyrics that expressed what I wanted to say for years. People who knew me got the message loud and clear.

After a few weeks back at the station it was made clear that this Monday to Thursday schedule had best be temporary. I was stuck in a position of unknowing. What ultimately would Shit Bag's sentence be? What about my mental health? There is no easy way to explain to upper management that I had come dangerously close to having a nervous breakdown, felt suicidal and hopeless. Completely alone.

Law enforcement didn't understand. My mother didn't understand. My employer didn't understand. Withholding one precious day of the week for myself at a company I had given everything to didn't seem like a diva request. I should note that if there had been the slightest interest in learning more about this trauma in the workplace and what it does to a person, my willingness to bend to their demands might've softened. It did the opposite. Every time Potsy dropped into conversation that I was receiving "special treatment" it only made me dig my heels in further.

Was I interested in personal appearances where I would be broadcasting my whereabouts without security? I'm going with NO.

Standing on your principles can mean shaky ground, as I soon learned they bumped me down to part-time status, pay cut and all. How fitting: now I'm being punished because I'm the only person interested in my own well-being. Throughout the entire ordeal it became almost mantra-like: I must be my own advocate. This was going to spill over into every area of my life.

I WAS SMOKING a heater on the patio at work, and a feeling washed over me that I have experienced maybe a handful of times before in my life. For a fleeting moment, I had a feeling of belonging. An assurance from the stars or the devil that this is exactly where I am supposed to be for now. I wish I could tell you that there was something profound that led up to this scene to make its power weightier. There's not. If I've learned anything, it is to grab those moments and RUN WITH THEM! They are just feelings that last a brief second, and it would be easy to be cynical and ignore them. Instead, store them somewhere; you'll surely need them again. Believe me, it's been so long since I've felt that my life has had levity; a moment of reflection that doesn't hurt or feel careless is worth everything.

When you've spent so long reaching for something out of your grasp, sometimes the hand that reaches back is your own.

27

SMOKING IN THE COURTROOM

Awaiting trial is like waiting for an execution.

You get told a date and try and psyche yourself up to face down the very evil that has put you in this wretched place of terror.

My god, where do I look? Do I have to use his actual name in court?

The day had finally come to give my impact statement in court. This is the first time I had a chance to speak about all this mental torture that started nearly three years ago.

When something is drawn out, rescheduled, and delayed, you can try and throw it on the pile with a host of everything else you can't control. Something is growing and intensifying within me. The anticipation of any kind of closure felt desperate and contingent on my mental health moving forward. This is my only chance to tell a judge with this Shit Bag in the same room what the impact of his stalking has done to me physically, mentally, professionally.

A deep fracture in my family occurred when neither my mom nor oldest sister had anything to say to me that didn't wound me. Their dismissiveness of how this was affecting me was remarkable. At my lowest. I was the proof. Gaunt, jumpy, and in rare displays of tears.

The cruelty in which they undermined the worst time in my life changed my boundaries with them forever.

The importance of chosen family was never more on display than each time I had to go downtown to the courthouse to meet with lawyers and victims' rights advocates. That routine of removing all metal objects, shoes, belts was tedious, and to look at the chosen friends who would assemble in my support was nothing short of magic.

When my story became public, I had a guy reach out to me that I had only known professionally asking what he could do to help. Naturally, people offer help in many instances, but you don't necessarily take them up on it or even believe that it's more than a token gesture.

This friend was active in his offer, and I remembered something that the victims' rights advocate had told me about having a large presence of supporters in court. I asked if he'd be willing to show up in court along with a well-curated group of true-blue friends.

MY SHRINK ADVISED ME to wear blue—there have been studies that apparently people feel they can trust what a person is saying when wearing this color. Think newscasters, politicians, airplane mechanics. Fun fact. I don't own a single item of blue clothing.

It should be noted that while my shrink was an amazing woman and therapist, she had moved out of state and our sessions were all done via Skype.

My workplace, trying to make a short leave of absence from work as bureaucratic and difficult as possible, was constantly bombarding her with paperwork to justify my leave on air and my lousy 50 percent salary.

She was getting frustrated that her work was becoming clerical rather than therapeutic. She did however point out one of the single greatest observations about me: I did not know how to breathe. Sounds simple, right? If you've ever been so riddled in knots and fearful, you probably know exactly what I'm talking about. On Skype she would stop me midsentence with the gentle reminder to breathe. She also scolded me repeatedly that I was drinking coffee during our sessions.

I'm truly grateful for her help and felt just as awkward when she would remind me of how much administrative work my employer was requiring from her. I'll admit it took my head out of the game as well. I'm not a fool, I realize I was paying for her time, but when things veered off into the matter of logistics and documentation requests, I projected that maybe she was losing interest in my situation.

Throughout our sessions she was always smart, kind, and available. Together we arrived at a major philosophy, which I still practice. Rather than the reminder to "stay positive," "stay curious" spoke to me on a different level. Learn to be curious about feeling the lowest lows and pay close attention to how you initially react. Accumulate the tools to navigate pain into a creative direction.

I'm not a keeper of journals, but at the very onset of this mess I began to instinctually write in a notebook. Actually, I had several notebooks going at once. I would scribble words as fast as they came to my head not caring about structure, legibility, or the idea that anyone other than myself would ever see these frantic writings.

The more powerless I felt accrued over so much time, I dug deep into my core searching to find anything resembling untapped strength. When the TV remote control isn't working, I always switch the batteries around and blow on them hoping to squeeze out the last bit of juice. I was checking my reserve tank daily. It took time, believe me, but I worked myself up to a place of anger and a refusal to accept that I would remain so emotionally paralyzed. I knew that writing a book about all of this stress would fulfill a creative need for myself. Creativity is a tangible source of power. I'd relied on it my entire life: why would now be any different? To be clear, I never thought what I would eventually write would ever help anyone else. I still wouldn't bet on it.

IT WAS DECEMBER 30, 2015. The closing of another year. That morning was freezing.

My amazing posse of rock and roll pals all showed up—not necessarily a group of early risers by nature. We met in front of the courthouse, stamping our feet to stay warm, and huddled into a small circle.

I had a chance to thank each one of them for giving me strength. I didn't ask any of them to do this. I will forever be blown away by their loyalty.

In no particular order, these are the all-star top-shelf friends who always showed up: Jess: toilet-cleaning bestie whose shared life and survival go beyond friendship, more like a creative collaboration. Abner: lifelong friend of the family, generous heart, and constantly stoned. My two brothers, Jim and Paulie. Ciaran: scrappy intellectual; headbutt first, ask questions later. Trent: my musical personality twin; we've never missed a Spoon show together. My darling brother Carlos who begins every single sentence with a curse word, e.g., "Shit I hope not." "Fuck if I know."

Steve: fellow dog lover. Lori: Mayor of Minneapolis Music; the baddest mamma jamma with the most tender innards I know; she's as quick to laugh as she is to cry. My sister Julie: a selfless giver who charmingly refers to my dogs and cats as her nieces and nephews. Mark: record store owner who offered his service of support out of thin air. Reed: a genuine rock star; throughout our friendship we always talk about writing. Ryan: if he started a cult, I would consider joining. Jill: work confidante; bought her four-year-old son a Shark vacuum cleaner for Christmas at his request. Mike: my pal Jade's father who at the creep's sentencing wore a T-shirt in court that said FUCK YOU, YOU FUCKING FUCK.

ONCE AGAIN, the nauseating ritual of shuffling through metal detectors, removing shoes, belts, and jewelry commenced. We waited for the last friend to pass through security, then we all jammed into one elevator. Nobody said much on the quick lift to the fourth floor. A couple of hand squeezes and understanding looks were exchanged.

Assembled in an office outside of the courtroom, we all stood awkwardly, nobody feeling the need to take a seat. Khaki Dockers gave a quick run-through of the proceedings. In my hand I was clutching my printed-out impact statement.

AT EXACTLY 8 a.m., we moved into the courthouse. Shit Bag was already seated ahead of us with his defense attorney. I took only the slightest glance at his orange-jumpsuited back, grateful not to see his face. I didn't need to see his face; it would be my voice ironically that he would hear as he had on the radio for years, only now for the first time being in the same room as my voice. My voice he had attached so many delusional ideas to. My voice he had built an entire imaginary relationship with. My voice that distorted any rational thinking in his mind. My voice he had made repeated threats to do harm to.

In the courtroom we sat behind the attorneys filling four rows of bench seating. I sat between my two brothers, one biological, one chosen.

The past two-plus years had led up to this moment.

The judge gave a stiff greeting and then a CliffsNotes version of the charges he was facing and about a sixty-second recap of what he had done. I scanned my friends faces; so much can be said with a simple look.

Standing in the very back I locked eyes with my police sergeant attending this hearing on her own time.

My heart was full.

> **COUNT I Charge: Stalking—Pattern of Stalking Conduct**
>
> Minnesota Statute: 609.749.5(a), with reference to: 609.749.5(a) Maximum Sentence: 10 YEARS AND/OR $20,000 Offense Level: Felony Offense Date (on or about): 06/12/2015 Control #(ICR#): 15226999 Charge Description: That on or between June 12, 2015 and June 20, 2015, in Minneapolis, Hennepin County, Minnesota, PATRICK HENRY KELLY engaged in a pattern of stalking conduct with respect to ML and/or members of the victim's household in a manner that would cause a reasonable

> person under the circumstances to feel terrorized or to fear bodily harm and that did cause this reaction on the part of ML

Before I stood up to walk to the microphone and read my statement, my brother Paulie crouched low and casually passed an e-cig to me. Even now I hesitate whether to share this detail, because of the absurdity and intimacy in that moment. Responding like it was the most normal and right thing to do in that moment, I ducked down and covertly took a rip on that thing and passed it to my brother Jim, who did the same.

That one act of instinctive solidarity touched me in a way that I still can't find words to adequately describe.

I had been kindly coached by Linda, the victims' rights advocate, that I could take my time while reading my impact statement. I could stop completely if overcome with emotion or have someone else read it for me. I wasn't nervous in the slightest. So much buildup provided me with the confidence to speak this truth aloud for the first time in front of a judge, my friends, and even the creeper himself.

The judge teed me up by acknowledging that I had something to say. My brothers and I stood and walked the short distance to the desk with the microphone. Seated between my brothers I read these words aloud in my voice:

> Good morning, Your Honor.
>
> The irony is that most people who hold a job in the public eye would describe themselves as being very private people. I am no exception. I've been in radio in this market for over twenty-one years; part of what makes me a good on-air host is my ability to connect to strangers. I've always employed a careful amount of transparency in my personality. I don't have a radio persona: there is no division between the Mary Lucia on the radio and Mary Lucia picking up after her dogs in the yard.
>
> I've always been passionate about my love of animals and have shared stories on air about my own pets and the struggles I've

faced in the pain of end-of-life decisions. It is not uncommon for listeners to reach out to me in their own times of pain, and I have always been more than willing to offer comfort and a communal sense that they are not alone in their grief. So to receive a random email from a stranger telling me his dog had died didn't send up any red flags. In my experience, one sympathetic response is usually all the further it goes. When the person persists in continually contacting me via emails, phone messages, letters, etc., that's when every siren goes off in my head; having had as much experience in radio as I have, it becomes clear pretty quick this person is boundaryless. All of these gestures are now unwanted, bothersome, and downright frightening.

In the spring of 2014, the endless stream of odd items being dropped off at the radio station by the defendant became very serious. Five pounds of raw meat, a photo of a man wearing a mask, children's toys, sympathy cards the kind you would send if a relative passes away, etc. Immediately, HR and Legal were notified. His email address and phone numbers were instantly blocked, and everything was sent to HR and Legal without me ever seeing anything.

Repeated behavior like this is threatening and invasive. I used to dread walking into work each day to see what new horror had been dropped off. I can't have my cell phone ringer turned on while I'm on air. One evening after work I saw that there was a phone message left from an unfamiliar number. I stood in my kitchen and heard this strange voice identifying himself as the defendant. The bottom of my stomach dropped out. My mind was reeling. How did this person get my private cell phone number, and if he got that information what else does he have? I didn't listen to the message in its entirety because my hands were shaking so violently. Instead, I let the St. Paul Police hear it the next morning. It was downright chilling; the tone of his voice was as if he was picking up in the middle of a conversation. Five minutes later I was walking down the street in St. Paul to file a restraining order.

For the next few days, I couldn't sleep or eat until I heard that the papers had been served to him.

It wasn't long after that phone call that I was at home in my dining room when I saw a man walk purposefully up my front walk to my front door; there was no hesitation, no looking for an address. Everything inside of me froze. Though I'd never laid eyes on him, I knew this was the man who has been stalking me and now he knows where I live! You can't imagine how terrifying it is to have the one place you should feel safe completely violated. After calling 911, I fled the house in the middle of the night to go stay in a hotel. I stayed in hotels on other occasions as well after he had been to my home.

The summer of 2014 I've never felt so unsafe or rattled in my life. I never opened a window, was constantly looking over my shoulder, jumping every time my motion lights went off, triple-locking all of my doors, sleeping with a baseball bat and cell phone. Every morning I would dread going out to the backyard to let the dogs out. He had been in my yard, my private sanctuary, leaving letters on my back sidewalk. For the record, Lebron James could not throw a letter over the top of my privacy gates and have them land perfectly positioned on my walkway in front of the back step facing up. It's simply not physically possible. Soon after, I got locks for the gates, and he did resort to hurling things over the fence.

My life became a sickening pattern of calling 911, collecting the evidence with plastic gloves and Ziploc bags, taking photos of the evidence, collecting my blue cards from the MPD, upgrading locks, installing security devices. And then I'd have to go work a full eight-hour day. I became afraid to do any sort of public appearances and my work started to suffer. I no longer felt comfortable being myself on air; revealing too much of myself became a constant concern.

I couldn't sleep or eat and have lost an unhealthy amount of weight and have been running to doctors endlessly. I've had stress-related painful shingles since May 2015. I've been in the emergency room with panic attacks. Simple joys have been taken away from me. I no longer feel safe walking my dogs after work. I've backed away from relationships, been forced to withdraw from society and this community that I love and am so familiar with. Suddenly, every stranger approaching you at a rock show feels like a threat.

When stalking like this goes on for months and months, it wears you down mentally and physically and changes you fundamentally. Your whole sense of self is in question. It's as if you suddenly wake up one morning and realize you've forgotten how to drive a car. Replacing all normal everyday thoughts with those of fear, dread, mistrust, and a general feeling of being unsafe anywhere. It's a horrible feeling to view both your workplace and home as a crime scene. The cost of this experience both personally and financially has nearly drained me. I'm most angered that a mentally unstable stranger has kept me from my career and altered my personal life to such a degree that I am forced to deal with it on a daily basis.

Post-Traumatic Stress Disorder is debilitating and can keep you paralyzed. This is an ongoing process of recovery. I have to fight every day to regain what I've lost.

In June of 2015 when I learned he had sent out at least six LinkedIn invites to my coworkers, my blood ran cold. I knew in my gut he would be back: sure enough, two days later he was at my front door. The complete brazen lack of regard that he was out on bail, has an active restraining order, and was awaiting an upcoming trial once again terrified me of his delusional intention to contact me at any cost.

Stalking is a horribly misunderstood crime; some people assume it's a "hazard of the job." Let me state for the record: no, it is not. To imply that is to suggest it is in some way acceptable and somehow not terrifying. It doesn't matter what is hand-delivered to your home—a candle, a basket of kittens, or a severed horse's head. The repeated violation of anything being left on your front step is creepy and indicative of a person so out of touch with reality that you don't know what else they are capable of doing.

Being stalked makes you feel powerless and helpless. This is not a domestic case of stalking, of which I believe law enforcement and the public in general have a better understanding. My story might be a bit more complicated than that. This is a complete stranger who has only heard my voice on a radio and through repeated reckless, delusional behavior has put me through the worst time in my life. Only twice in the past year and a half have I felt as close to safe as I'll ever feel, and that has been both times the defendant has been locked up in jail. He has proven time and time again that if left to his own judgment and compliance with restraining orders and bail orders, he simply CANNOT leave me alone. He clearly has no regard for the law or awareness of the toll his crime has taken on me.

I don't know him. He doesn't know me. He will never know me. If he makes one more attempt to contact me, I hope he realizes that he is ruining his own life, and for what?

My best hope as an outcome of this miserable experience is that he receives the maximum jail time, the maximum supervised probation, and a mandatory mental health treatment plan.

Thank you.

Author: KARE 11 Staff
December 30, 2015

MINNEAPOLIS—The man who pleaded guilty to stalking The Current DJ, Mary Lucia, was sentenced Wednesday.

Patrick Henry Kelly, 56, was convicted of making terroristic threats against Lucia, forcing her to take a leave of absence from her job in April. According to authorities, Kelly became obsessed with Lucia, repeatedly visiting her home and leaving notes and keepsakes, despite a restraining order barring him from doing so.

> On Wednesday, Kelly was sentenced to 270 days at the Hennepin County workhouse. However, he did get credit for more than 190 days that he's already served. He was also sentenced to five years of supervised probation with conditions, including that he is not within 10 blocks of Lucia's home or workplace. He was then ordered to pay restitution of more than $9,000.
>
> Kelly was released Wednesday morning, because of time off for good conduct.
>
> Lucia attended the sentencing with her two brothers. She gave her victim impact statement, describing how she lived in fear because of Kelly's actions.
>
> "I never opened my windows," she told the court. "I jumped whenever the motion sensors went off. I triple-locked my doors. When I went to bed at night, I slept with a baseball bat and a cell phone near me."
>
> Lucia said she couldn't sleep or eat. She had panic attacks that would send her to the hospital and felt threatened anytime a stranger approached her.
>
> "My whole sense of self is in question," she said. "It has left me feeling powerless."
>
> Lucia announced her return to The Current airwaves in November, saying the ongoing stalking situation turned her life upside down for the last two years.
>
> "I won't lie, I've been knocked around quite a bit and been forced to accept things I still find unacceptable. I've felt lost and powerless," she wrote to her fans and listeners.

So that's it. Other than that, Mr. Lincoln, did you enjoy the play?

A slap on the wrist and probation. Time served awaiting trial was in the plus column for him. Good conduct? What the shit is that? As far as financial restitution, that's a laugh.

Intellectually, I had plenty of time to evaluate the kind of mind that has no regard for the law, a person's safety, or privacy. Facing jail time means nothing. They have nothing to lose. Their delusion is so real there is nothing to stop him pursuing me. He is convinced we are in love and that I think of him sexually. His illness sees him as a protector and predator. Something terrible is going to happen to me, by his own hand, and yet he ultimately will be the only one there for me. The courts can't mandate mental health treatment. Best they can offer is parole, a stern warning, and the proverbial, "I don't want to see you back in my courtroom ever." Which might be affective if we weren't dealing with serious mental illness. He's proven that the story in his head is as real as my trauma is to me.

It was a sick realization that law enforcement's idea of someone being a danger or posing a credible threat required that I have a gunshot or stab wound on the outside of my body to prove actual harm had been done.

The damage was there, just not outwardly for people to see. I'm sure it sounds overly dramatic, but I can attest to the internal beating and scarring. Your sense of power has been shredded. Feelings of safety blown to smithereens. You will profile strangers on first impressions. PTSD is a beast.

Like many things, there isn't a cure. It's all about managing these responses. Like addiction, you are now in recovery mode.

His ultimate sentence felt like nothing.

Knowing that after this hearing I would walk out of the courtroom trusting that I had been heard by the judge, my pain held value and weight.

There was little comfort in his flaccid sentencing: a five-year probation for a mentally unwell man. A serial stalker whose warped version of reality was never going to be professionally addressed or treated. He would walk out of the courtroom a free man. The same man who sat in the orange jumpsuit with his back to me while I spoke was on the street a few hours later, expected to understand his crime and the toll it took on a complete stranger.

28

SHIT BAG RETURNS

PUTTING DISTANCE FROM THE PERSON I WAS FIVE YEARS AGO HAS been an ongoing struggle. I can see that paralyzing fear and the feeling of being powerless have morphed into a righteous anger. Anger is an energy. Thanks, Mr. Lydon.

One way I have replaced the feelings of helplessness is to honor that rage I feel inside.

Imagining him back on my property, I follow through the thinking of what weapon I'm going to strike him with. I have quite the arsenal. Louisville sluggers. Helpful tip in the interest of efficiency: put a sock on the end of your baseball bat so that when you swing for his fat skull, if he should try and grab the bat from you, he'll grab the end with the stocking, and it will slip off leaving you open to take another crack.

Fireplace poker, mace, a cue ball in a sock. Not a crew sock, a knee-high, that way you don't have to stand as close to num-chuk the shit out of his face.

I'VE COME A LONG WAY. It took almost two years before I could give my current boyfriend a key to my house.

I still have a crap-ton of triggers. (If there was a less-used word, I would use it.)

Please don't ever leave ANYTHING sitting on my front step. Even if it's a basket filled with Pug puppies. My heart still catches in my throat when I see something on the stoop.

I don't like the initial sight of hand-addressed mail.

I still jump at loud noises, which I never did before all of this. I'm hesitant in crowds and have learned an initial quick scan of the room helps me do a ten-second profiling of potential weirdos.

A stranger telling me I smell nice does not mean they want to poison my dogs. Nor should I mace them.

Unknown callers on my phone will never be answered.

I still occasionally engage in self-harm. I know, I know, and smoking causes cancer.

While thrifting I bought a cool old sofa. I had to tell them I'd come back to pick it up, so they started writing up a sold sign and asked my name and number to post on it.

Without hesitation a fake name and number came tumbling out of my mouth.

FOUR YEARS HAD PASSED when through the paper-thin office walls I heard Potsy on speakerphone and clearly heard both my name and a coworker's in his loud conversation.

Casually, I brought it up to her, asking if she knew any reason why we'd be lumped together into a conference call. Somewhat reluctantly my coworker told me she had an unwanted visitor stop by her house.

I knew instantly where this was going.

I knew. I knew. I knew.

SHE SHOWED ME a vague image captured on a doorbell camera. I only had to take a cursory glance. It was him.

My heart was broken, knowing what she was about to go through.

Upon learning of his reappearance, I immediately went to the courthouse and applied for a fifty-year restraining order. These are not given lightly.

Knowing what I knew, the restraining order is the first order of protection and at the very least you've begun the paper trail. You feel proactive for about a minute until he repeatedly violates the order, which he will. Also from experience, the confusion and hoop jumping that goes with the order of protection being served thus making it valid still makes me furious.

She was in the early stages of this criminal's obsession with her. She is a thoughtful woman and I believe didn't want to share too many of her fears out of concern that I would be right back where I was a few years earlier. I respected her process but also felt that, Jesus Christmas, we have been stalked by the same person at different times. Our collective information could be powerful and could maybe even shorten the time of his harassment.

Never once did I think, I'm glad it's not me. Because it is me. It's her. It's you. It's me.

It didn't feel right to ask any real specifics with her.

How did it start? Did he come right to her home? Had there been emails, letters, raw meat bouquets?

I tried to take her lead and not involve myself in her case. I admit it felt peculiar.

Learning bits and pieces of her situation didn't tear open a festering wound. It bears repeating: I never truly considered this to be over.

It put an awkwardness into our relationship. I never saw this as two stand-alone incidents.

Yes, we are different women, but are we really able to look past the fact that all of this stress was being perpetrated by the same individual?

Also reinforcing the impotency of the system that relied on him to check in regularly with his parole officer.

Digging around I found that he almost immediately dipped on his five-year probation check-ins from my case. He was declared indigent and without any known address. Lost in the system.

Four years later, technology really boosted his arsenal of harassment. Burner phones were the new thing. Untraceable phone numbers.

This dope dropped a burner off at her home doorstep encouraging her to communicate privately with him this way.

My concern and curiosity had to take a back seat to her privacy. I wanted to ask so many questions. Was it fair to assume I knew how she felt? Had he changed up any of his tactics? How often was he intruding on her life? Did she have a plan for personal security? Could we somehow Thelma and Louise it and take care of him once and for all?

This time I started thinking outside of the law. Vigilante-type shit. You know it's serious when you start to dream about playing dodgeball with people's severed heads.

I asked her for the license plate number and make of his car.

Knowing that I had to be my own advocate, I did my own sleuthing to find out where he was living. The wind was nearly knocked out of me when my police friend came up with a last-known address as being two stinking blocks from my house!

That was chilling and more than likely in violation of my new and improved restraining order.

I wasn't going to involve her in anyway, but I wasn't going to take this passively. Underscoring my disbelief in the adage, Everything happens for a reason. I don't accept it. It feels way too passive to swallow.

In the undercover of darkness, I trolled his block looking for his car. How does this shit bag afford to drive a Lexus is beside the point: who is bankrolling this predator? What I may or may not have done next was grab a wrench from my trunk and methodically walk to his parked car and bust out his taillight.

My rationale was hopefully the cops would have no problem pulling this car over without a working taillight, and maybe they'd run his name through the system, see his outstandings and warrants, and my friend would be that much closer to him being locked up, even if temporarily.

Let's be real: I was doing this for both of us. I couldn't tell anyone what I'd done. Now I'm telling you.

I felt a sense of exhilaration and danger. I was feral. You'd be surprised what trauma can make you do.

It also felt righteous and warranted.

It was not lost on me that I was engaging in criminal sneaky behavior not unlike . . . I don't know . . . say, a stalker.

I HAD THE FIFTY-YEAR restraining order, so I contacted the company's lawyers that were hired to help my friend. Explaining that he is clearly in violation of my order of protection. The attorney I spoke with began to explain, sounding oddly rehearsed, that technically he was something absurd like 50 feet beyond the jurisdiction of where I lived. She used some crow's flight analogy that immediately irritated me. It was clear that the company was involved to help my friend and my previous case seemed to hold no bearing.

While I was grateful that they seemed to be offering some support to my colleague, I couldn't help but think of how I was left twisting in the wind on my own a mere four years prior. Knowing their main concern is company optics, it made sense that I was the guinea pig and now they couldn't look inept with the same lunatic stalking my coworker.

My colleague informed me that her lawyers served his restraining order by publication and were able to convince him to turn himself in. He was in temporary custody now. I knew exactly what she must've felt. Maybe the first good night's sleep in months. Hope that the history of his repeat offenses would stick. Real jail time and meaningful consequences that matched the terror she was put through.

My cynical inner ghoul had other thoughts. We were dealing with mental illness. Thirty days of lunchmeat sandwiches in the clink wasn't going to magically serve as mental rehabilitation.

I kicked into rage overdrive. While doing my daily show I found his current mug shot online and began to assemble my own version of a WANTED flyer of warning that I planned to stick to the big glass door to his apartment building and anywhere else in the vicinity. Printing it out at work I huddled over the printer, guarding the contents of each page being spit out. I included all of the charges he was currently facing and those he had previously avoided. I wanted the landlord to know that this is the type of person they were renting an apartment to. Also, any women residents might be interested in knowing that this repeat offender was using the same laundry room.

After work I parked half a block away. It was daylight saving time, dark, and also high Covid time. I had my mask on and my hood. I plastered the big entrance door top to bottom. I know that one flyer might've sufficed, but thinking if someone entering their apartment building saw it, they could easily remove it. But if there were twenty-five covering the entirety of the door, the statement would look crazy enough to warrant some attention.

Looking into the vestibule and seeing his pathetic name on a mailbox, wondering how many official court documents and warrants had been placed into the slot, was an odd feeling.

After the deed was done, I circled back just to see if anyone had entered. The door remained wallpapered with his face.

As twisted as all of this might sound, feeling helpless for so long, anything I could do that didn't reek of victim felt proactive.

I circled that block plenty. I'm not even certain why.

I learned bits and pieces of her case and offered more than once that if I could help in any way, she could count on me.

Her lawyers made it clear that I should not be involved in any way.

It all felt sickeningly familiar: at one point she mentioned he requested to act as his own attorney. One advantage was there weren't any court cases being heard in person—it was all Zoom hearings. She wouldn't even have to be in the same room or look at the back of his head.

He ended up with the exact same sentencing as in my case. Time served and probation.

I DON'T REMEMBER EXACTLY how much time passed before he was at it again with her. At the time of writing, he was deemed mentally incompetent to stand trial. Awaiting some halfway house arrangement and then a reassessment of his mental health. A pattern of ten years of convicted felony stalking is going to fall through the cracks. I will never be able to make that right in my head.

The system is deeply flawed. Do I accept that? Never.

There were plenty of times in which I was made to feel that the predator's privacy was of greater importance.

I don't have the energy or wherewithal to take up the fight to change laws.

I don't want to be the face of stalking.

As far as my former coworker's case this is still unresolved and ongoing. Which means that all parties affected by his behavior and illness over the years will drag this jive around until we can't any longer. I've been changed. My eyes are open, and if it's a healthy dose of anger I need to feel slightly less powerless, so be it.

What should be emphasized is the broken system is allowing yet another person to experience the fear of being hunted.

I'll leave all of that here, as it is her aching story to tell.

29

FOR THOSE ABOUT TO SALUTE, I ROCK YOU

In early March 2020, I was on air when an urgent all-staff email came through proclaiming the Covid-19 virus had reached pandemic status and that all employees not on air should immediately evacuate the building.

The mass exodus of every person working on my floor grabbing random things from their desks and fleeing was unsettling to say the least.

There I stood in my glass soundproof fishbowl wondering what this would mean to those of us hosts who held regular time slots. I felt like a musician on the *Titanic.*

Confusion and a profound alteration in our work as a radio station were the new uncertain reality. This job would never be the same again.

To be considered an essential worker at first sounded a little theatrical. However, the first few months we realized how many people were either out of work or lucky enough to be working from home relying on connection through their favorite radio station, which gave us a real feeling of purpose to what we did. Masked up with raw hands from constant hand washing and scrubbing down the console and studio nightly with bleach became routine.

This meant a building that had formerly been bustling was a ghost town overnight. Building ops thought this would be the perfect time to save on heat and electricity. Adding to the dystopian feeling of having only six people inside the building, we were doing our jobs in relative darkness.

That's great for morale. This was also the optimum time to get some pesky structural problems repaired, with walls being ripped out and air ducts being torn into. Every day I passed the same wrangler jean ass halfway up a ladder in the middle of the hallway with his head in the ceiling.

The women's room toilet was clogged for a few months. I sent building operations a notification a few times. Finally, their solution appeared in the form of a plunger.

Sorry, you don't pay me enough.

CALLING IN SICK was not a possibility. Shorthanded and unvaccinated, we who were expected to be there running the store had to use every resource available to acquire the first available shots. This was way before you could schedule an appointment at CVS. People were road-tripping to Walmart in northern Minnesota, or like me I had some weird intel about a makeshift pop-up clinic offering Moderna shots out of a storefront in North Minneapolis.

This strangely apocalyptic way of working had been operating about two months before the entirety of the world was laser-focused on our hometown. Memorial Day 2020 George Floyd was murdered in the street in broad daylight by the MPD. A cacophony of broken hearts and spirits crashed over our city. The collective grief was felt in everything you saw, whether it be on the nightly news or stepping out of your front door.

It was surreal watching the news and seeing Anderson Cooper reporting from the streets in front of my burned-down post office.

Curfews were established, and suddenly I had to have a media badge on me at all times to drive on the roads to get to and from work. Road closures, daily protests, helicopters, National Guard tanks, and daily warnings of people throwing bricks off the freeway overpass had replaced garage sales, street fairs, and music in the parks.

We had a huge target on our backs, being the biggest liberal news outlet one block from the State Capitol. Windows got boarded up and we had security on each floor at every exit.

Everything was charged with emotion and injustice. Peoples' righteous anger spilled onto every street. Stay-at-home orders only seemed to bottle up the powder keg of outrage. As far as my job went, I tried to be more mindful than ever in the songs I selected to play for my four-hour show. Everyone doesn't feel the same way: how do you express and represent that division through music? That in itself was a creative challenge I felt proud to tackle. Speaking to the almost mystical power music holds, I think more than anything, I felt a bond to listeners that was different than any other time in my career. I was grateful to be experienced and able to think quick on my feet because now more than ever this was an absolute need during this time.

Playing a thoughtful set of tunes you hoped something would resonate with someone, and quite often it did. Bill Withers, Run the Jewels, Sam Cooke, and Childish Gambino did a lot of healing that summer.

With time, as more CDC guidelines changed, lucky us the managers were allowed back into the building to work. With only a small handful of us being on the fourth floor, we naturally spread out and began working from the unused offices of employees now working from home.

When asked why I wasn't working from my desk, I reminded management of social distancing and pointed out that the only four people in the building were all in the same cube quadrant/sneeze zone, which made no sense when more than half of the building was unoccupied.

Imminent conflict hung in the air. "Hello unnecessary micromanaging my old friend, I've come to talk with you again." Here we go, the house is on fire, but let's not run out of the burning building: let's stop to dust the coffee table.

The people who were really holding down the fort were all women. Morning, Midday, Afternoon. Potsy didn't trust the experience and professionalism of any of us. After all we did for that station, selling that corduroy and making it swing.

I had just as much actual radio experience as he did. That I had established my reputation and credibility in this town seemed to get under his skin. Rather than celebrating it, I was condescended to. My caliber of consistent work, which should've been my currency, was still less than men who worked fewer hours on air. Having given everything to a company, including my personal safety, was handled with a demotion and a pay cut. It never sat right with me and never will.

So many strong talented women had left the company: it was a daily reminder of how undervalued we were made to feel. Everyone is replaceable.

One woman, a successful published author who was hired as a writer for our digital content, was eventually told, "Nobody reads. Make videos instead."

So much dumbing down without a collective mutiny was too much to carry on my shoulders alone.

Believe me when I tell you I tried.

THE COURT SENTENCING DAY of former MPD Derek Chauvin was being carried live on my broadcast. I was a mess with emotion and feelings of unease, which I couldn't express in this news-based noneditorializing institution. Potsy texted me with this message: "Make sure you have the right songs queued up ready to go after the verdict is announced. EITHER WAY."

Say what, now? What does *either way* mean? If he had gotten off, should I have NWA in the queue?

GOING IN DAILY was becoming a brain drain. I couldn't help but feel that between the gender pay gap and incompetency of management it was rendering this job unhealthy for me.

Around the time of the January 6 Capitol insurrection, I started to white-knuckle it.

During the Covid lockdown, I admit to feeling envious of coworkers that sat in Zoom meetings looking relaxed in their drawstring pants, cats sauntering across their keyboards. Masked up at the company's headquarters with my glasses continually fogging up, my anxiety tote bag was gradually filling with unhealthy resentment.

I had to be certain that I had exhausted every possible avenue to create a more fun and equitable workplace. Never underestimate fun. When you accept that fun has left the building, I don't see the nobility in hanging on, feeling frustrated and undervalued. The realization that the change I so wanted to see from others would ultimately have to come from me, at first, left me feeling defeated.

After twenty-eight years working in the cock-a-doodle-dude world of radio, I took a gamble that I might be great at something else (results still pending). Resigning became my plan.

I knew I was going to be crafting an at-home recording studio. I asked one of the lifer audio engineers how best to do it. I crap you negative his response was, "Go to a U-Haul truck rental and steal their blankets." I'm not a criminal, but thanks anyhoo.

IT WAS FAR MORE EMOTIONAL than I had anticipated signing off on my last show.

I had made a public social media post about my leaving the radio station prior to the last day in the booth. A local reporter had left a few messages for me, but I didn't respond. Finally, reaching a well-respected former coworker for comment, she told them, "Just listen to her show: Looch has always said what she needs to say with the music she chooses."

After being a founding creator of this radio station, I was escorted to the lobby and reminded to leave my pass key ID badge on the desk. Or I'd be charged twenty-five bucks.

What, no sheet cake?

Within seconds of leaving the building my phone blew up. I was wiping away tears and ignored the notifications, assuming it was my friends who had been listening. What it was in reality was half of my coworkers relaying that at 6:01 p.m., an all-staff email was sent out that Potsy was no longer an employee of the company.

Translation: CANNED.

Did I see that coming? Nope. Do I understand why they let me quit? Nope. Is the timing incredibly confusing? Yes.

I can honestly say corporate decisions are not for me to understand.

ANYTHING THAT FEELS like it's holding your integrity hostage must be kicked to the curb. Remember every time you feel the system is trying to bury you, they are burying your seed of ideas.

Holding on to pain and trauma will hold you back to some extent—that's a given. I'm still struggling, trying to compartmentalize these negative experiences knowing it is with purpose. The act of writing this book is new and exciting territory.

I'm grateful that the dream I'm chasing is authoring a memoir. Seems lofty but within my reach. For whatever auspicious reason I have the confidence that I've got the goods to back this shit up with a compelling story and unique perspective. Like anything else, when sticking my neck out the hope is this will land and connect in front of someone who gets me. I know what a genuinely rare thing that is, as it's been my guiding belief in this whole endeavor.

I'm forever ready to find someone just as dark and dirty as I am to find humor in terrible things that will afford me the chance to flop or take flight.

With the frustration there is also a thrill that no matter what you've put out creatively in the past, plunging forward into an entirely different arena, being judged by people who are looking at what goods you are coughing up in the NOW with no regard for previous accomplishments, feels like reinvention.

Knock, knock. Who's there? Mary Lucia. Mary Lucia who? Exactly.

THROUGHOUT my professional career I have always had great empathy for those who seek recognition for their music, submitting personal work to various radio station clowns, record labels, and clubs. The worst kind of cold-calling to the nameless and faceless. Hoping some renegade spirit will hear the value in their songs and follow up with a prompt response that will allow them to take another step closer to their rock and roll dreams.

Realizing the beauty of your music is in the ears of the beholder.

A single person's disinterest is not the end. You will continue to take crap gigs performing in front of twenty people. Swallow the expense and put out your own records.

Write on. Realizing, ultimately, the world owes you nothing, but it's okay to secretly believe it might. Especially if your karma bank is full and you know you have something new to say.

I've seen and heard you for years. I'll always relate to you.

I will appropriate that same rock and roll spirit in this new chapter of my career. Accepting no as an answer while allowing for the possibility that someone I haven't encountered yet holds a precious yes.

I will always be more interested in your stories.

Time and experience have honed my desire to cut through the bullshit. Can I put that on a résumé?

I WAS RECENTLY APPROACHED to be a part of a "Where Are They Now" article.

Holy Thursday, Batman!! Not even two years out of my radio gig? I'm now qualifying for this kind of has-been recluse feature?

With a tightened sphincter I responded with, Really? Will you also be featuring the local pedophile restauranteur who's been lamming it in Mexico, and the kid from *The Shining*?

Where am I now?

I'm still here.

AN OLD RADIO TROPE we're all taught is to imagine you're talking to one specific person. I took that recommendation and distilled it down still more to match my intention: I imagined the one person out there receiving my voice and vibe was exactly like me. It *was* me. The way I could assume my taste and humor were always understood. I love this music. You love this music. I want to hear the answer to this inane question and so do you. When hitting a wall in an interview, my go-to question was: If you lost your arms from the elbow down in some freak accident, you would only have two options: (1) go without any appendages; or (2) have Chihuahua paws surgically attached and live that way. Which would you choose? Naturally, there is a correct answer. I could tell so much about a person by their initial reaction to being asked this seemingly left-field inquiry. Then my heart would grow when they began to seriously consider a life with tiny paws and sharp little black nails click-clacking across wooden floors.

Funnily enough, it turned out to be you.

Play "Misty Mountain Hop" for me.

EPILOGUE

My Mom Is Coming Home to Die

My mom is coming home to die.

We've been circling the drain for so many years. I've often laughed at the thought that she's hung on for spite. There really doesn't appear to be anything substantive to keep her here. Though I could make a case that the Twins baseball broadcasts being yanked unceremoniously hasn't helped much in her will to live.

Once again, I think of the unreasonable expectations we place on the dying to accommodate our own emotional limitations.

Expect the unexpected and you won't be disappointed. Since her multiple strokes last week, we've had several plans that have changed on a dime.

Visiting her in the hospital and seeing her lifeless body looking tinier than ever. The detached part of our expected real relationship as mother and youngest daughter kicks into overdrive and I simply see her as a human being suffering. Every past transgression and hurt feeling dissipate like the left side of her paralyzed frail body.

She lies in the hospital bed like a stoned burrito. Eyes closed, moaning, stretching her one mobile leg with carefully painted toenails.

I do the only thing I know and that is to stroke her hair and massage her scalp like I would one of my pets. An intimate act that hasn't been approached in more than thirty years.

My siblings fumble around with their true feelings, knowing that in the end she will get what she wants. She always has. Why should it change now that she is fading?

Some hold on to feelings of frustration that spill out as misplaced anger at the attending physicians. Others simply stay away from the uncomfortable reality.

I sit in no judgment of my brothers and sisters, as we are all strong unique personalities perhaps cultivated by the woman herself lying helplessly in the bed before me.

Something that still makes me laugh was a time when we were kids, and two siblings were arguing over something foolish, and Hal just bellowed into the other room, "HANDLE IT!!" Handle it we will. Between the four of us combined we make one fairly capable person.

A HOSPITAL PRIEST VISITS while we're there. Personally, if it were me, I would find this terrifying. I'd rather someone bring an intuitive cat into my room to officially tell me I'm dying. I fixate on his bloody bandaged finger holding rosary beads. It's all I can do from advising him to elevate it. Embarrassed that we no longer can recite certain prayers, we bow our heads awkwardly and hope that he will leave the room before seeing we are all ambiguous spiritual beings at best.

We've been anticipating this in our own different ways for so long, and to fault someone for their personal grief response, the one that feels right to them, feels pointless.

Stop drinking poison and expecting the other guy to drop dead has been a mantra in my head.

Things aren't going as we would have liked or planned, and, in an instant, you have to get yourself right with life's relentless curveballs.

Things get stripped down to the basest level of understanding. Tenderness amongst ourselves will go a long way, I believe.

Are we equipped to care for her in her home with only a faint grasp of reality left in her usually sharp mind? Oh hell no.

I would expect nothing less.

Before entering the hospital, did she leave the faucet in her bathroom sink running all night enough to cause severe water damage in the floors and basement? Yes, she did.

Are the hired dudes who are coming to fix it bumping up against the exact time she will be transported back home in a hospital bed to finish out her last days? Absolutely. Does this add to the absurdity? You better believe it.

Did we have a half-baked conversation about what room to put her hospital bed in, considering that her living room is the most spacious but also has a large picture window in which the mail carrier can see us changing her diapers? Christ you know it. My gallows humor can't help but tease my oldest brother, who remains at a distance, that I envision calling and informing him she's miraculously made a full recovery and insists she can only go on living if it's at his bachelor crib.

This woman will do whatever she wants, defying logic or reason, and the sooner we get on board in accepting that the better. Nobody can tell her what to do even with multiple strokes on both sides of her brain. We as her children have no pull. I have often thought that a random handyman fixing her gutter could offer some life advice that her inner Blanche Dubois would take as gospel.

Right before I left the hospital room after sitting there for hours, all the while her eyes remained closed, no words of substance were spoken. A handsome nurse came in to adjust her slumped body in the bed; she appeared to be shivering. He asked if she was cold and that he could bump the thermostat up if she liked. With my own ears I heard her reply, "Okey dokey."

I don't know anything.

Hospice brought her home to die in her home on a Friday. I was there every day.

Her eyes never opened, and she could no longer swallow. Having lost 99 percent of her hearing, previous face-to-face encounters involved yelling, overenunciating, and some finely-honed charades skills. I was told that the hearing is one of the last senses to go, even in a person who relied on hearing aids. This was a gift. I could speak in my normal tone of voice. I chose to believe she could hear everything being said.

Lying there in her TJ Maxx floral nightgown, her face looking remarkably unlined and expressionless.

She was wearing a few rings on fingers that were swollen at the knuckle. I was told I could call a local fire station to cut the rings from her fingers. Making that call felt surreal. I didn't know they offered that particular service, so cautiously I explained that my mom was at home hospice and was wearing several rings that appeared to be cutting off circulation. They told me to call 911, as every truck wasn't equipped with the proper tin snips. I thought no more fire engines, ambulances, and other emergency vehicles needed to hurtle down her quiet street.

I began the ritual of speaking closely to her face encouraging her that we were all there. (We weren't.) We would be okay. (We aren't.) She was going to be okay. (Eh?) She no longer had anything to worry about or feel frightened of and that she could let go. Stop struggling, stop hanging on. Relent.

Nobody can prepare you for what is known as agonal breathing. Trying to separate the thought that this was just a physical response to shutting down and not her fully conscious mind unable to let go.

Morphine is something of a miracle drug. Helping both the dying and the living to alleviate concerns of real pain and discomfort. Reading all the hospice pamphlets of what to expect near the end. I held out hope that there would be one more "rally" in her before passing away. Suddenly clear-eyed and in full voice, requesting fried chicken while criticizing what I was wearing.

It was not lost on me that over the years I had tried so hard to get her help in many ways to address the difficulties of her past. Here I was again in a very different way to offer what little help I could.

My own relationship with ML was coming to an end. Right here. In her stuffy pale blue bedroom. There would be no more shouted conversations or birthday gifts to buy her affection.

So much sadness for what could have been dying with her.

I'd been dragging this weight around way too long. The idea of being untethered seemed possible for the first time. For both of us. Could we both be free? This was a brand-new thought, one in which I took some comfort.

The next carefully timed morphine dose finally turned the page. The precarious space of simultaneously living and dying.

I'm sorry, ML, that it took so long to arrive here.

I'm here.

It would be lovely, and not to mention a good book ending, if this also dovetailed neatly into the raggedy trauma I still lug around from being stalked. Could I also one day be free of that?

I'll clasp my tiny Chihuahua paws together and try my best to stay curious that anything is possible.

LAST SHOW PLAYLIST
MAY 12, 2022

Keith Richards, "Take It So Hard"
New York Dolls, "Personality Crisis"
Guided by Voices, "Motor Away"
Patsy Cline, "Strange" (Live)
Jenny Lewis with the Watson Twins, "The Big Guns"
Billy Idol, "Can't Break Me Down"
The Vaccines, "Blow It Up"
The Redwalls, "Hung Up on the Way I'm Feeling"
Kathleen Edwards, "Sidecar"
Faces, "Pool Hall Richard" (Single Version)
Dolly Parton, "Mule Skinner Blues (Blue Yodel No. 8)"
Motörhead, "Ace of Spades"
Cher, "Believe"
Spoon, "I Turn My Camera On"
Sam Cooke, "A Change Is Gonna Come"
Stiff Little Fingers, "Alternative Ulster"
Sparklehorse, "It's Not So Hard"
Mavis Staples, "99 and ½"
Willie Nelson, "Funny How Time Slips Away"
Louis XIV, "Illegal Tender" (Album Version)
Dave Edmunds, "Crawling from the Wreckage"
Sweet, "Little Willy"
Aerosmith, "Lick and a Promise"
Neil Diamond, "Brother Love's Traveling Salvation Show"
Margo Price, "Pay Gap"

T. Rex, "Hot Love"
All, "Dot"
The Replacements, "I.O.U."
Starcrawler, "I Love LA"
Tony Bennett and Count Basie, "Are You Havin' Any Fun?"
Badfinger, "Rock of All Ages"
The Beatles, "Blue Jay Way"
Mount Moriah, "Lament"
Tom Jones, "Green Green Grass of Home"
Robert Plant, "Rainbow"
Eagles, "Heartache Tonight"
Glen Campbell, "Gentle on My Mind"
Brendan Benson, "What I'm Looking For"
The Clash, "I'm So Bored with the U.S.A."
Prince, "D.M.S.R."
John Mellencamp, "Hurts So Good"
Slade, "The Bangin' Man"
Nick Lowe, "So It Goes"
Etta James, "Trust in Me"
The Spinners, "I'll Be Around"
Charlie Sexton, "Beat's So Lonely"
Visqueen, "Crush on Radio"
The Subways, "Rock & Roll Queen"
Queen, "Bohemian Rhapsody"
Little Man, "Shag If You Want To"
The Jayhawks, "Don't Let the World Get in Your Way"
Bee Gees, "Run to Me"
Dead Kennedys, "Kill the Poor"
Richard Ashcroft, "Why Not Nothing?"
The Walkmen, "The Rat"
INXS, "What You Need"
Terry Reid, "Speak Now or Forever Hold Your Peace"
Tom Petty and the Heartbreakers, "Shadow of a Doubt (A Complex Kid)"

The Velvet Underground, "Cool It Down"
Lissie, "Best Days"
Madonna, "Express Yourself"
Frank Sinatra, "My Way"
David Bowie, "Heroes"
The Rolling Stones, "It's Only Rock 'n' Roll (But I Like It)"

ACKNOWLEDGMENTS

ERIK ANDERSON MY EDITOR WHO WAS THE FIRST PERSON TO SHOW interest in my story years before I was able to tell it.

Sergeant Darcy Horn of the Minneapolis Police Department. The only law enforcement official to offer empathy and humanity. Linda from Hennepin County Victims' Advocates who spent so much time on the phone with me and never made me feel nuts. Belinda who talked me off the ledge weekly via Skype. Dr. Walker who actually gave me her home phone number.

My family.

Julie who used to rip shitties in winter parking lots with me as a kid.

Carlos who begins and ends every sentence with profanity.

P.DUB my big brother who always knows when to rally.

Hal who spoke his own language that I could always discern.

Abbie Kane (Li'l Abner) my sister and most treasured friend. Jessica Hanson my bestie who I plan to grow old and weirder with.

Jim Boquist my chosen brother who has a way of speaking in which everything feels important. Lori Barbero (Captain Hooker) whose huge laugh is matched by the size of her enormous heart.

My courthouse crew who rolled deep with me all the way.

Mike, Trehus, Trent, Ciaran, Traster, Jill, Steve, and Reed.

Pedro Juan, Katie Dohman, and Spoon.

My former radio partners in crime. Jade, Derrick, Perkins, Kelsey, Wiza, Cecilia, Leah, Wheat, Jill, Andrea, DeVille, Mackenzie, Emily, Brett, Luke, DeMark, Sean, and the one in a million Bob Collins.

Joseph Gallup a true gentleman rogue.

MARY LUCIA is an acclaimed broadcast personality, writer, audiobook narrator, actor, and voice-over artist based in Minneapolis. She hosted a variety of on-air radio shows, including local music show *Popular Creeps* and, for nearly two decades, for Minnesota Public Radio's The Current as the afternoon-drive host. She now works as a program advisor at Radio K, the University of Minnesota's renowned student-run radio station.